Get Weller

SOONER

12 Powerful, Proven Ways to Speed and Improve Your Recovery from Illness or Surgery

Stan Munslow

GET WELLER SOONER
12 Powerful, Proven Ways to Speed and Improve Your Recovery from Illness or Surgery

Cover: Angie@Pro_Ebookcovers and Umarch4

IMPORTANT NOTICE

Dedication

For all who suffer from illness or surgery, and for their loved ones who suffer with them. May the words and healing energy in this book help you to see it through with strength, wisdom, and equanimity.

Table of Contents

Preface

"Natural forces within us are the true healers of disease."
Hippocrates

"The body creates health daily. It is inherently self-healing."
Christiane Northrup, M.D.

I must confess I find it rather sobering to realize that I am writing a book for people who, to put it bluntly, feel like crap.

And you're one of them, aren't you? Either that, or perhaps you have an upcoming surgery, chemotherapy infusion, or some other treatment—*after which* you plan to feel like crap.

But most likely you are in the hospital right now—recovering from surgery or being treated for illness—and you chose a book with the title "Get Weller Sooner," because that's what you would like more than anything else right now: to stop feeling like crap, shuck off that johnny, and go home.

And the sooner, the better.

Well, let's assume (and hope) that you are receiving excellent care. You have the best doctors, nurses, and technicians working on your behalf. You have the latest treatments, medicines, and high-tech medical equipment at your disposal. If so, that's wonderful!

And yet, wouldn't it be even more wonderful:

- If you could accelerate the healing and recovery process and return to your normal, healthy life sooner?

- If you were to experience less pain and fewer complications while recovering from illness or surgery?

- If you could improve your prospects for healing from a serious illness?

- If your body were to respond better to the medications or infusions you are receiving, and with minimal side-effects?

- If your out-of-pocket costs were reduced as a result of any of the above?

In other words, wouldn't it be just plain better if your entire medical experience turned out to be *just plain better* than what you and everyone else, including your doctors, were expecting?

Healing better, healing faster—in other words: getting "weller" sooner—of course you want that. Who wouldn't?

Well, in just a moment, I'll explain exactly how this book is going to help you get there.

But before I do, we need to be clear about a couple of things:

First, I am not a doctor, and this book is in no way whatsoever a substitute for licensed, professional medical care. It is a *supplement* to it. And although it offers no guarantees, you are absolutely doing the right thing for your body and your overall well-being by infusing its teachings into your mind, body, and spirit.

Second, many of the healing strategies you are about to learn can boast more than a few well-documented success stories involving individuals who achieved amazing results, even complete cures, using nothing but one specific strategy alone. Nonetheless, I warn you, I urge you, and I implore you to do no such thing! Use any or all of these methods only as a *supplement* to regular professional care. Use them *in conjunction with* standard medical care. Use them to *optimize* and *enhance* the success of your surgery, the outcome of your treatments, and the efficacy of your medications.

Use them to *augment* and *build upon* your care, not replace it.

I cannot stress this enough. If you are to get weller sooner, you need to explore *all* avenues of healing, of which this book represents only a part.

To illustrate, let me share with you an example from my own life:

Back in the late 1990s, my dad, at age seventy-five, was diagnosed with stage-four lymphoma and given a thirty-percent chance of survival. Well, he went the standard route of working with an oncologist and receiving chemotherapy.

Meanwhile, desperately unwilling to accept the thirty-percent survival prognosis he'd been given, I immersed myself in a ton of research on health and healing. Then, I distilled the most valuable information from this research down to a pocket-sized healing guidebook for him to carry around, along with a cassette tape of healing visualizations and affirmations to aid in his battle.

So, you see, my Dad did both: He did his chemo, *and* he worked with his homemade healing materials. He carried his little book with him wherever he went and read it over and over.

He even read it while he was receiving his chemo. And he listened to his cassette every day.

In the end, my Dad beat his cancer. And by that, I mean he went beyond remission and achieved full recovery.

But here's the miraculous part: My Dad didn't just beat it. More like: He *sailed* his way to beating it. He had a far better experience with his chemo than anyone expected. He didn't lose his hair. He didn't lose weight. He didn't get nauseous. He remained positive, upbeat, and active. He responded to his treatments better and faster than was typical, especially for a man of his age and with cancer as advanced as his.

Were that little book and cassette contributing factors? Well, all I can say is there wasn't a person in my Dad's life who didn't firmly believe so.

Well, one might ask, would he have achieved the same success *without* the chemo? Goodness, of course not.

On the other hand, would the chemo have worked without those other things? Yes, I'm quite sure it would have.

But here's the big question: Would the chemo have worked as quickly, as easily, or as effectively without them?

Even my Dad's oncologist's reply: an emphatic *no*.

To this day, we, the members of his family, regard his outcome as nothing short of miraculous.

And it gets even better for *you*.

This book has *far* more to offer you than what my Dad had. In fact, let me tell you a bit about how this book came to be, and how it will help you to get weller sooner:

I've always had a deep interest in science, especially *quantum* science, and I've read many books on the subject over the years. But after doing further research following my Dad's amazing recovery, I realized that there was so much more potential healing to be had—for anyone in the family, or among our friends, who happened to need it.

So, in the years that followed, I began to refine and expand upon the methods I'd used with my Dad. Next, I began to offer them to anyone I knew who was facing serious illness or a big surgery.

And from there, the successes began to rack up:

- A close friend had major abdominal surgery and was told she would be out of the hospital in nine days. She was out in five.

- Another friend, in poor health to begin with, underwent a surgery that promised to be tricky at best, risky at worst. He was out in ninety minutes and thrived fabulously afterward.

- At eighty-four, my Mom suffered a massive stroke. It was so bad she wasn't expected to make it through the night. Thankfully, she did—and then went on to enjoy a recovery so astounding that, within months, she was even doing crossword puzzles again.

- My sister-in-law was diagnosed with stage-four ovarian cancer. Now, nearly five years later, she continues to respond to her treatments and live a normal life.

Meanwhile, as I moved through my forties and fifties, I became increasingly aware of yet another "success" taking place, this one concerning my own medical status:

I wasn't getting sick—as in: *ever.*

Throughout my adult life, I've suffered no illness whatsoever, save a lackluster bout of flu in 2005, which lasted all of thirty-six hours. Nothing else. Not a thing. And I've enjoyed perfect health to this day, having just celebrated my sixtieth birthday. I've never been hospitalized. I've had no surgeries. I've developed no chronic aches, pains, or conditions throughout my entire life. I rarely see a doctor. And I remain very strong, active, and vital.

What is the "secret" of my success? Well, it sure isn't genetics. Both my parents and four siblings have had, shall we say, a "typical" life of various illnesses, conditions, and medical misadventures. Scratch genetics.

Some would say I've been "lucky"—to which I would respond: "Lucky? For *sixty years straight*? Seriously?"

True, I've exercised my entire adult life and maintained a healthy diet along the way. These are perhaps modest contributors. But I know perfectly well what the biggest reasons are:

First, I never *expected* to get sick. I still don't. Frankly, I don't expect or anticipate a single medical problem for the rest of my life. I'm certain of it. (See Chapter 3 on the power of positive expectation.)

Second, for many years, I've operated from the conviction that my body is perfect, and I know full-well that this thinking greatly impacts what goes on inside my body (see Chapter 1 on the power of the mind-body connection).

Bottom line: I live by these principles and others that you will find in this book, and my results speak for themselves, as do the results of people I know who have gotten weller sooner than anyone expected.

And if a day should come when I find myself hospitalized for some reason, I intend to use every single method in this book and rack up yet another success because that is precisely what I will *expect* to happen.

Now, let's talk about *you*. How can this book help you to get weller sooner?

First, you are going to learn twelve powerful healing methods, culled from the cutting edge of medical science. These twelve strategies will provide you with new understanding, new habits, new techniques, and new beliefs that will power up the ability of your mind to affect healing throughout your body. They will also offer you specific strategies, practices, and techniques to help you heal faster and better than with conventional treatments alone.

Each has the potential to improve and accelerate your healing and recovery process. But when used together, you'll have a veritable powerhouse of healing energy working on your behalf.

And there's more:

Each chapter will also provide you with twenty-five powerful *affirmations*, which will drive the key points and healing energies deep into your mind and body.

And here we have the most striking feature of this book, one which sets it apart from all other books on healing. It is a methodology I've been using for years, in many different applications.

I call it *"Learn & Affirm."*

It's very simple: You learn something, then you repeat powerful and positive statements on the subject over and over until they are driven firmly into your subconscious mind and their healing energy spreads throughout your body.

I'll explain this process in detail in Chapters 1 and 8.

The use of positive affirmation is one of the primary techniques my Dad used, and it is one of the most important ways by which the greats from all fields achieve success. I invite you to join them.

You're in for an amazing journey of healing with the power of affirmation.

Finally, each chapter will conclude with three specific action steps you can take to further aid in your healing and recovery process.

But I know you want to get weller *very* sooner. So, enough prefacing. Let's get started on your healing journey right now.

1

Get Weller Sooner with the Power of Your Mind

"Our body is shaped by our mind, for we become what we think."

Buddha

"E = mc²"

Albert Einstein

I understand. Really, I do. You feel like crap and reading a book—any book—is probably the last thing you want to be doing right now. But please do read it, or at least ask someone to read it to you, because, in some way, large or small, it *will* help. I mean that. These pages contain more ways to help people feel better than you can shake a thermometer at. So, hang in there; I promise it will be worth it.

So, what's your story? Are you awaiting surgery? Recovering from surgery? Fighting an illness? About to undergo a major procedure? In the midst of some other form of medical misfortune?

In any case, it's safe to say you're not a happy camper right now, and I'm sure you could find better things with which to fill your day than pain, nausea, weakness, beeping monitors, and your roommate's blaring TV game-shows.

It's also safe to say that there is just one thing you want more than anything else right now: to get well soon.

Well, sure, getting well is a wonderful thing. And it is a good start. But how about going beyond "well"? How about getting well-*er*? Wouldn't that be a whole lot better than just plain "well"?

And, yes, "soon" is a good start, too. But how about getting well *sooner* than "soon"? I mean, wouldn't soon-*er* be a whole lot better than just plain "soon"?

So, yes, how about *getting weller sooner*? How about getting well more quickly, more easily, and more completely? How about getting well with less pain, fewer side effects, and fewer complications along the way?

Ah, to get weller sooner! Seriously, wouldn't that be a whole heaping lot better?

Well then, in order to increase the likelihood of this welcome outcome coming your way, your first step is to understand and acknowledge the true depth of what has become known as the *mind-body connection.* This term refers to the incredible influence and control your mind has over your body and its prospects for more rapid and thorough healing, not to mention your prospects for remaining healthy afterward and possibly living a longer life.

Thanks to discoveries in the field of quantum physics, we are now coming to understand that our thoughts not only *affect* the body ...that our thoughts not only *control* the body...but that our thoughts—to an almost unfathomable degree—literally *create* the body.

Our thoughts not only affect and control the body, they create the body.

Now, take a moment to open up your mind nice and wide and let those words really sink in. This is such a profound concept that, at first, it's almost impossible to wrap one's brain around it. Our bodies are, quite literally, the result of our own thinking far more than most people realize—indeed, far more than you could possibly imagine.

Your thoughts—that is, your habitual and deeply-held thoughts, beliefs, and expectations—largely create the conditions within your body:

- They help to improve the durability and functional capability of new cells (which your body creates at the mind-boggling rate of some two million per second).

- They determine how well your body can fight off illness.

- They decide how quickly and completely your body can heal from illness.

- They affect how soon you will recover after surgery.

- They regulate your overall level of health and well-being in lockstep with your deep-seated beliefs and expectations regarding your overall level of health and well-being.

How? Well, here is what quantum science can teach us and, more important, how you can harness this knowledge to help improve your prospects for rapid healing and a complication-free recovery process:

First, as you are well aware, your body is made of cells—some thirty to forty trillion of them. And, as you may remember from high school chemistry, these cells, like all matter, are made out of molecules, which, in turn, are comprised of atoms.

But what you may not know is that these atoms, and all other atoms throughout the Universe, are actually comprised of nothing but *energy*—tiny, vibrating bundles of energy. Yes, energy. That's it. That's what atoms are and that's *all* that they are. This is what Einstein's Theory of Relativity is all about:

$$E = mc^2$$

"*E*" (energy) equals "*m*" (mass; a.k.a.: matter) times "*c²*" (the speed of light squared— a staggeringly fast speed).

To put it more simply: Mass *equals* energy. Matter is *made* of energy. All things (and that includes *you*) are made of energy. They may appear solid, but this is an illusion brought about by the dizzying speed at which the energy vibrates.

So, all appearances to the contrary, your body is made of nothing but energy.

Your body is made entirely of energy.

Surprisingly, this astounding fact has been part of science for over one hundred years. But here is an even more astonishing fact, brought to us by the good folks who work in the field of quantum science:

If matter is made of energy, what, then, is energy made of?

Answer: (Get ready for this!) Energy is comprised of *awareness*—of i*ntelligence*. Your body, like everything else, is *made* of intelligence.

The energy that makes up the cells of your body is comprised of intelligence.

Chew on this for a while. Mind-boggling, isn't it? But, rest assured, it has plenty of good, solid science to back it up.

Just consider these words from the late British physicist, Sir James Jeans, courtesy of *Moral Technologies*:

"The Universe begins to look more like a great *thought* than a great machine. Mind no longer appears to be an accidental intruder into the realm of matter; we ought rather hail it as the *creator* and governor of the realm of matter."

Or this, from *Conscious Reminder:*

"Physicists are being forced to admit that the Universe is *mental construction*."

Which I would modify to: "...the Universe *and everything in it—including your body—*is mental construction."

Is it starting to register?

I won't bore you with the scientific hows, whys, or wherefores of all this. But, if you're curious, just Google what has become known as the famous "double slit experiment" and read to your heart's content on the shocking scientific research that led to this rather jaw-dropping conclusion.

For now, suffice it to say that your *thinking* literally creates your body. When you get right down to it, it is what your body is made of. And, most important, your thinking is lord and master to everything that goes on inside you, including your ability to heal and recover more quickly and completely.

And your thinking creates the conditions within your body, as it always has, *whether you understand and acknowledge this fact or not.*

It's just that, under your conscious and positive control, you can do a much better job of it.

This, my friend, is the true miracle of the mind-body connection.

I know; I understand. It is so hard to fathom that this could be true, and yet it most certainly is. It is real. It is science. And it has been proven scientifically time and again. But it isn't necessary for you to understand the mechanics involved with this. All it takes is for you to acknowledge this blessing and act upon it.

And this is the premise upon which much of this book rests: Your body *is* made of intelligence. And this means that:

1. Your thinking controls your body.

2. Your mind *creates* the very cells of your body, and it causes those two million new cells your body creates every second to be healthier (or unhealthier), stronger (or weaker), and more effective (or less effective) at what they do.

3. Your thinking—your thoughts, beliefs, and, most important, your *expectations*—are what cause your body to be *what* it is and the *way* it is.

So, if you want to get weller sooner—and stay that way—you must first understand that you *are* what you think; you are *literally* what you think.

And with this knowledge comes incredible healing power.

Knowing that your body, including its healing and recovery, stems from your thinking means that you have very real power over your prospects for getting well faster and out of the hospital sooner. Your body will largely heal as quickly, or as slowly, as you *think* it will. Your body will heal as well, or as poorly, as you *expect* it will.

Your body will largely heal from illness or surgery as quickly and as completely as you expect it to.

Want proof? Consider "the placebo effect": a proven phenomenon that occurs when a patient's *expectations* cause a certain medication to work, even if the "medication" turns out to be completely fake.

This means, for example, that if you are given a sugar pill and you are told that it is actually a powerful pain medication, your belief (your thinking) regarding its alleged "efficacy" will generally bring about the same reduction or elimination of pain as would a "real" pain medication.

Even more astounding is what can happen to people with multiple personality disorder. In

Quantum Healing, Dr. Deepak Chopra explains that when a person with this condition shifts from one personality to another, their *physiology* shifts with it.

For example, if someone is allergic to orange juice, they will likely break out in hives when they drink it. But when they shift to another personality, the allergy and their resulting hives disappear.

Or, if a patient has, say, non-insulin-dependent diabetes, which requires them to take a drug to maintain their blood sugar levels, and then they switch over to another personality, they no longer need to take the drug because their pancreas is now functioning normally.

Now, is that incredible or what?

These phenomena clearly demonstrate the incredible power that the mind has over the body.

And so:

- If you *expect* to heal quickly, you are more likely to do so. So, do it. Take ownership of what goes on inside your body: *Expect to heal quickly from whatever illness you have or whatever surgery you've undergone—and don't let up.*

- If you are certain that you will have fewer side effects from medications or chemotherapy, you most likely will. So, do that, too: Remain certain that you will have minimal side effects (or none at all) from whatever medications or chemotherapy you are receiving.

- If you routinely *assume the best* in regards to your healing or recovery, you are more likely to heal or recover faster and better. Yes, do that as well: *Always assume the best in regards to your healing or recovery.*

- If you believe—*really believe*—in the incredible power of your mind to help your body heal faster, recover more completely, and remain healthy ever after, you are helping to make it all happen. *Yes, believe with all your heart in the incredible power of your mind to help your body heal faster, recover more completely, and remain healthy thereafter.*

And this is where *affirmations* come in.

As I've explained, you *are* what you think you are. Your body *is* what you think it to be. And your health is as good as you *say* it is. Your habitual thoughts, beliefs, *and statements* about your body have an unbelievably strong impact upon your health and your ability to heal from illness or surgery.

For good or bad.

Your statements about your body have a strong impact upon your ability to heal.

If your thoughts, beliefs, and *statements* about your health lie mostly in the negative, the disempowering, or even the self-destructive categories, your body *will* listen. And somehow, at some time, these statements will likely manifest within your body in the form of chronic or frequent illness, as well as diminished prospects for healing and recovery from illness or surgery.

The good news is that the opposite is every bit as true. If you feed your body a steady diet of healthful, empowering, and positive thoughts, beliefs, and *statements*, your body will listen to those as well. And it will respond accordingly.

And if you send your body a steady stream of messages in the form of powerful and positive statements—*which you repeat emphatically and often*—those thirty-plus trillion cells that make up your body will really sit up and take notice!

These positive statements are called *affirmations*. And here is the feature which really sets this book apart: You're not merely going to learn how to recover better and heal faster, you're going to infuse your brain with the very messages it needs in order to help bring about improved health, rapid healing, and effective recovery throughout your body.

> *The use of affirmations will help to infuse your brain with the thought-energy it needs to help bring about rapid healing, and effective recovery.*

As I mentioned in the preface, this book utilizes my unique "Learn and Affirm" system. In each chapter, you will learn a powerful, proven healing technique or strategy (such as calling upon the power of your mind to take control of the body and help make you well). Then, at the end of each chapter, you will discover twenty-five carefully crafted and powerful affirmations, which, when repeated silently or audibly, will begin to infuse your thinking with the healing energy it needs most to set your mind and body on a direct path toward rapid healing with less pain and fewer complications.

The use of affirmations is very widespread among people from all walks of life, from actors and athletes to pop singers and television personalities (Jim Carrey, Michael Jordan, Jenifer Lopez, and Oprah Winfrey, to name a few). It is widespread because affirmations are very powerful and effective in bringing about a desired outcome.

> ***Affirmations are very powerful and effective in bringing about a desired outcome.***

What's even more important to understand is that, if the use of affirmations is so effective in acting upon outside circumstances, such as the generation of wealth or success, imagine what they can do for the goings-on inside your own body!

This is important, so let me repeat:

If the use of affirmations is so effective in acting upon outside circumstances, such as the generation of wealth or success, imagine what they can do for the goings-on inside your own body.

This means that the beliefs you hold about your body—and the repeated messages you send it—have a significant impact on your well-being. And the more than three hundred affirmations presented in this book will begin to feed your mind-body the messages it needs most to return you to top working condition very soon.

Now, please understand that, by using these affirmations, you are seeking, most of all, *improvement in your condition*. You are not necessarily going to cause every statement you make to come true right away or to the same extent you would like. Repeatedly affirming: "I am now healed" won't necessarily cause you to become completely healed overnight; it means that, at the very least, you are helping yourself to become healed *more* quickly and *more* completely. And that is, ahem, nothing to sneeze at.

Don't worry if you don't believe some of these statements at first. Just allow the words to seep repeatedly into your subconscious. In time, you will come to see that your health and well-being are in your hands far more than you could ever have imagined. Affirmations work. Affirmations work wonders. And on the next page, you will begin to discover some of the very best affirmations your body could ever know.

Affirm the Healing Power of the Mind-Body Connection

Read the following affirmations, silently or aloud, *with conviction and feeling*. And, please, read them often—the more often, the better. If you are not up to the task, ask a friend or loved one to read them to you, or, better yet, record them (on a voice-memo app on your cellphone) for you to listen to at any time of day or night. (Yes, even while you are asleep; your subconscious mind will continue to receive and act upon their healing power all through the night.)

Feel them, absorb them. Use that powerful mind of yours to visualize these affirmations as they infuse your every cell with the very wisdom they convey. See them filling you with their power. Feel them filling you with their healing energy.

1

My body is made of cells. My cells, like all matter, are made of energy. *My body is made of energy.*

2

Energy, according to quantum science, is made of awareness—of intelligence. In truth, my body is made by my intelligence; it is made by my *thinking*.

3

My positive thoughts, beliefs, and expectations work to help bring about my good health, and this includes my speedy recovery from surgery or illness.

4

My mind creates my body. My thoughts, beliefs, and expectations strongly impact my body's creation of new cells, as well as the ability of these cells to keep me healthy.

5

My habitual thoughts regarding my body help determine the overall conditions within my body. I think good health, not illness. I think strength, not weakness. I think recovery, not relapse. I think wellness, not illness.

6

I am *literally* what I think I am.

7

My body is what I continually think it to be.
Therefore, I think only the best thoughts
regarding my health and well-being.

8

My body is healed by my continual thoughts of
healing, and I understand that this truth is
based on hard science.

9

My body is made strong by my continual
thoughts of strength, and I understand that
this truth is based on hard science.

10

My body generates healthy, perfect new cells
every second. In my mind's eye, I see millions
of healthy, perfect cells being created right
now.

11

I am what I think. I think health, strength, energy, and vitality—always. Therefore, I *am* healthy, strong, energetic, and vital.

12

When I am ill, I don't focus on the illness. I focus on wellness. I focus on getting strong and getting well. I repeatedly visualize what it will feel like to be well again.

13

I think health and well-being—always—and I will have them.

14

I steer my mind away from fearful thoughts about "prolonged illness," "relapse," or "possible complications." I understand that these possibilities exist and, should any of them arise, I will act upon them. But I need not make a habit of sending such toxic energies into my body.

15

I don't anticipate illness. I don't expect to get sick. I don't expect to remain sick. I continually anticipate my continued good health—and I will have it.

16

If I shift my attention away from any pain or discomfort and focus, instead, on feeling good again, I will get more of the same: I will begin to feel good.

17

If I shift my attention away from any pain or discomfort and focus, instead, on feeling good again, I will experience less pain and less discomfort.

18

I often visualize all the parts of my body as perfect—as functioning perfectly—whether they are at this moment or not. My body listens to my thoughts. What I think I become.

19

I see my body not as it "appears" to be, but as I *want* it to be. I understand that this is the way of highly successful individuals: to continually focus attention not on the way things are, but on the way I want them to be.

20

My beliefs and expectations about my body are a much stronger determiner of my health and healing than luck, fate, prior medical history, or even genetics.

21

Every part of my body—every organ, gland, bone, muscle, tissue, and cell—is now functioning perfectly as it receives the energy of my continued thoughts of healing, wellness, and good health.

22

My positive thoughts about my body are, at this very moment, creating my very being—my very healthy being—for what I think, I will become.

23

My thoughts are energy. My body is energy. My thoughts of strength and wellness are now merging the energies of strength and wellness with the energy that makes up my body.

24

The energy that stems from my thoughts of wellness is now infusing the cells of my body with the ability to help bring about wellness and rapid healing.

25

I accept, acknowledge, believe in, and embrace the proven power of the mind-body connection to aid in my healing process.

Healing Actions

Here are three things you can do, starting today, to help enhance and empower your own mind-body connection. In so doing, you will strengthen your mind's ability to bring about more rapid and complete healing within your body.

1. Understanding
Take a few minutes right now, and at various times throughout the day, to marvel at this incredible truth: *Your body is made from the energy created by your thinking.* This gives you great power over your body's natural healing process. Dwell on this. Meditate on it. Be in awe of your power.

2. Visualization
Begin making a habit of imagining powerful healing processes going on inside you. Picture your organs, your tissues, and even your cells becoming healthier by the hour. Picture your body healing perfectly from the surgery. Picture your illness quickly receding. Picture these goings-on in bright, living color, and with as

much detail as you can. Do this often (more on visualization in Chapter 3).

3. Expectation

From now on, expect nothing but success for the duration of your hospitalization, treatment, or convalescence. Expect a successful surgery or procedure, successful healing from illness, and a successful recovery. From this moment forward, expect nothing but optimum health and wellness for your body.

2

Get Weller Sooner with the Power of Positive Thinking

"Keep your face to the sunshine, and you cannot see a shadow."

Helen Keller

"Find a place inside where there is joy, and the joy will burn out the pain."

Joseph Campbell

By now, I hope you've come to understand and acknowledge what a crucial role your thinking plays in affecting, controlling, and even creating the conditions within your body, including its ability to help your body to heal.

Consider these statements from Dr. Joseph Mercola (mercola.com):

- Positive thoughts are able to prompt changes in your body that strengthen your immune system, decrease pain and chronic disease, and provide stress relief.

- Happiness, optimism, life satisfaction, and other positive psychological attributes are associated with a lower risk of heart disease.

- It has even been scientifically shown that happiness can alter your genes! A team of researchers at UCLA showed that people with a deep sense of happiness had lower levels of inflammatory gene expression and stronger antiviral and antibody responses.

Keeping Dr. Mercola's words in mind, if you want to speed up and enhance the process of getting well, your next step is to create an *optimal healing environment* within your body. You do this by making sure that your thoughts about your body, your illness or surgery, your hospitalization or treatments, and life in general, remain as positive as they can be.

Your job throughout your healing and recovery process is to *continually* fill your mind and spirit with positivity in all its forms:

happiness, joy, delight, contentment, jubilation, hope, exuberance, exhilaration, elation, confidence, euphoria, gratitude, enchantment, enthusiasm, blessedness, optimism, humor, lightheartedness, serenity, and bliss (to name a few!). Doing so will infuse your body with the energy it needs to heal quickly and heal well.

The power of positive thinking cannot be denied nor overstated. Positive thinking works, plain and simple. It heals. It strengthens. It cleanses. It empowers. So, even though you cannot expect to be positive and upbeat one-hundred percent of the time, it is imperative that you do all you can to make positive thinking and positive *feeling* your primary states of being—*even when you are sick or in pain*—indeed, *especially* when you are sick or in pain.

> **Make positive thinking a habit even when you are sick or in pain—especially when you are sick or in pain.**

What this means is that, by *choosing* to entertain continually happy and uplifting thoughts (while doing your best to ignore or tune out any pain, weakness, or apprehension you may be experiencing), you are sending powerfully positive energies into your body. In so doing, you are creating a physiology and an immune system that is bolstered, invigorated, and strengthened by these energies.

You read that right. You ignore, to the best of your ability, any discomfort or distress you may experience during your illness or recovery period. You just plain ignore it. You do this by *choosing* positive thoughts, focusing on them, and even dwelling on them. You don't give yourself a chance to go negative. You give your attention to positives and nothing but positives.

Energy flows where attention goes. If you focus on pain; you'll get more pain. If you focus on negative feelings such as worry, apprehension, weakness, gloom, and doom, you will infuse your body with these debilitating energies.

If instead, you focus on healing, you will steer your body in that direction. If you focus on positive feelings such as serenity, gratitude, and strength, you will fill your body with these empowering energies.

Granted, when you're sick or in recovery, staying positive can seem almost chore-like. Worse, many people simply feel justified in suffering when they're ill or in pain, and that includes *thinking* about their suffering. So, they focus all their thoughts on the pain, often thinking it is their "right" to do so, and they will even shout out their cries of despair to anyone who will listen.

If this sounds like you, let me ask: How is that working for you? Is all the negative talk helping your body or your spirit in some mysterious way? Do you prefer to *focus* on the pain, thereby noticing it more, feeling it more, experiencing it more, and possibly deepening and prolonging the pain itself?

Wouldn't you just rather get weller sooner and get yourself out of that freaking hospital?

To put it another way: While you may have every "right" to suffer, this doesn't mean it is in your body's *best interest* to give over your attention and energy into doing so.

Focusing on negatives such as pain does not aid in the healing process. Focusing on positives does. Focusing on wellness does.

If you want your pain, discomfort, weakness, apprehension, or general displeasure to lessen, get your mind—your thought energy—off of it. If you want to heal faster, get your mind onto any thoughts that make you feel good.

See, you are not thinking happy thoughts because they make you happy. At this moment anyway, you are thinking happy thoughts because they make you *healthy*.

Happiness heals. Humor heals. Gratitude heals. Positive thinking in all forms helps to lessen the severity of an illness and shorten its duration. Look it up. You'll find plenty of data attesting to this.

> *Positive thinking helps to lessen the severity of an illness and shorten its duration.*

However, in order to maximize the effectiveness of positive thinking, you must go beyond simply entertaining positive thoughts. You must *feel* them! You must feel them to your core. You must feel them tingle their way into every corner in your body—even the parts that hurt.

Furthermore, you must bring yourself to a place where you wholeheartedly *believe* in the proven power of positivity to help your body get well. Remember, our bodies are created by our thoughts. If your thoughts are continually upbeat and filled with positive energy, your body will respond accordingly. Likewise, if your thoughts are frequently unhappy, fearful, or focused on pain, your body will, again, respond accordingly.

So, no matter how uncomfortable you may be during this time, I urge you to focus on all the good you possibly can. Right now:

- Recall happy memories from your childhood: wonderful vacations, amazing adventures, and magical moments.

- Think of your friends and loved ones. Be grateful for all that they bring to your life.

- Ruminate on a time when someone was proud of you or especially kind to you.

- Think about your first kiss. Or, if your spouse or partner doesn't approve, think about your first car.

- Be grateful for all you have. Count your blessings—all of them—then count them again. No matter what your present situation may be, there are *always* a million-and-one things to be thankful for.

- Dwell upon any successes, large and small, personal or professional, that you've had in your life.

- Recall something silly that happened recently.

- Reminisce about a fabulous movie you've seen recently.

- Focus your awareness on any parts of your body that are *not* affected by your illness, or are not in pain.

- Find something, anything, to feel good about and do all you can to keep your thoughts there. Need help? Go to: www.wisebread.com/big-list-of-things-to-be-happy-about for an enormous list of happy thought-starters. That should keep you smiling for another fifty years or so.

Now, in case you may be thinking that it is not within your power to adopt a positive mental attitude at will, especially when you are suffering, know full-well that it most certainly *is* within your power! It is *your* mind and you are free to utilize it in any way you want. You are free to choose and entertain any thoughts you wish, whether they are positive or negative. You are free to think on or dwell upon any subject you like, at any time you like. You are free to focus on positives any time you like, particularly when it is in your physiological best interest to do so.

You are also free to ignore any negative thoughts that arise—to gently but persistently replace any and all negative thoughts with more positive, healing ones, and to diminish the power and the "drama" we often attach to our negative thinking ("catastrophizing") merely by *choosing* to do so.

It is within your power to adopt a positive, healing mental attitude right now.

So, make the good choice. Put reminders on sticky notes such as: "P.M.A EVERY DAY!" or ask someone to do it for you. (P.M.A. stands for Positive Mental Attitude.) Type a similar message as an hourly alarm or reminder on your phone or tablet. Ask your nurse to write cheery happiness reminders on that wipe-off board facing your bed. Ask family members or friends to bestow you with positive-minded phone calls, texts, and in-person reminders.

And don't forget to remind everyone to keep any negative thoughts they may have about your situation to themselves!

Last but not least: *Smile!* Whether you feel like it or not. Smile at everyone you meet, whether they return the smile or not. Smile for no reason at all. Smile in the dark when falling asleep or at times in the night when you can't sleep. Just smile. This one act, done often, will do more for your physical and emotional well-being than any self-help book ever written.

It's true: The physical act of smiling actually signals the brain to release happiness-inducing chemicals. Study after study bears this out. Sure, being happy makes you smile; we all know that. But scientists have discovered that this works in both directions. Being happy makes you smile and smiling makes you happy—even if you weren't all that happy beforehand.

Here's how *Scientific American* puts it: "A spate of recent studies suggests that our emotions are reinforced—perhaps even driven—by their corresponding facial expressions."

And this, according to *Psychology Today*: "Most people think that we smile because we feel happy, but it can go the other way as well: We feel happy because we smile."

So, wipe that smile right *onto* your face this instant, whether you feel like it or not. Smile at your nurse. Smile at the person in the next bed, even if they're grouchy. Smile at the sunshine streaming through the window. Smile at videos of silly dogs or cats on Facebook. And smile for no reason at all.

Your brain will take it from there, and then send the good news to the rest of your body.

Your body will take it from there and send the good news to your doctors and loved ones.

Affirm the Healing Power of Positive Thinking

Read the following affirmations, silently or aloud, *with conviction and feeling.*

1

I understand that, since my body is made of energy, when I infuse it continually with positive energy in the form of joy, gratitude, and positive expectations, my healing is improved and accelerated.

2

Even when I have an illness occupying one part of my body, I continue to regard the rest of my body as completely healthy.

3

To the greatest extent I can muster, I remain happy, upbeat, and full of positive energy throughout my illness, both to lessen its severity and shorten its duration.

4

Smiling is good for my physiology. No illness has the power to keep me from smiling. I am smiling right now!

5

No illness is stronger than my positive attitude, my upbeat spirit, or my unshakable hope.

6

I am fully aware that my positivity, happiness, and upbeat spirit will help to mend my body to the extent that I *believe* in its power to do so.

7

To my core, I believe in the power of positive thinking, and I've got modern science on my side to back up this conviction.

8

When illness comes into my body, I focus my attention not on the illness, but on all the good that is in my life: family, friends, pleasurable activities, happy memories, successes, and blessings.

9

When illness comes into my body, I focus my attention not on the illness, but on those parts of my body that remain healthy and unaffected by the illness.

10

When I am ill or recovering from surgery, I focus on being well—on the *feeling* of being well—as often as I can. I visualize being well, using all my senses and with deep, tingling emotion.

11

Whenever I am sick, I smile, I laugh, I think positive, uplifting thoughts, and I keep my mind off the sickness.

12

Whenever I am sick, I spend my quiet time recalling happy moments from my life, big and small.

13

While in the hospital, I spend my quiet time counting my blessings over and over. I have so much to be grateful for, and I take none of it for granted.

14

I am happy. I am joyful. I am delighted. I am content. I am hopeful. I am grateful. I am enthusiastic. I am blessed. I am optimistic. I am lighthearted. I am serene.

15

My body tingles with the energy of happiness that I am now feeling.

16

My chosen feelings of happiness and joy help return my body to a robust and vital state.

17

My chosen feelings of enthusiasm and exuberance help return my body to a strong and healthy state.

18

In this life, I generally don't take things—including myself—too seriously.

19

The cells of my body operate at peak performance when they are infused with my positive thoughts and feelings.

20

Happiness and a positive outlook are choices. They are decisions. And I choose to remain happy throughout my illness or hospitalization.

21

I expect, fully and intensely, that my chosen positive thoughts and feelings will do wonders for my healing and recovery.

22

I understand the power of gratitude. I understand that the Universe gives us more of that which we are grateful. I give thanks for all my blessings, including any healing I may have experienced in the past.

23

My positive mental attitude has tremendous power to keep me healthy, especially when I wholeheartedly believe in this power.

24

Right now, I am sending a steady stream of positive thoughts into my body, strengthening it with their powerful, healing energy.

25

I accept, acknowledge, believe in, and embrace the proven power of positive thinking to aid in my healing process.

Healing Actions

Here are three things you can do, starting today, to help foster and strengthen the proven power of positive thinking in helping your body to heal:

1. Positive Thought

From this moment forward, allow no negative thoughts regarding your body, your health, or your healing and recovery to take up long-term residence inside your head. When a negative thought does arise, gently push it aside and replace it with something uplifting.

2. Positive Talk

No more negative talk. No moaning or groaning. No blaming or complaining. No doomsday statements about your body or your health. Keep your language as upbeat and hopeful as you possibly can.

3. Positive Action

Smile! As much as you possibly can. Find something to smile about throughout your day. Smile because, when it comes to your physical well-being, you have *every* reason to do so. Remind yourself that the act of smiling itself sends signals to the brain to bring about feelings of happiness. These, in turn, send positive, healing energy into your body.

3

Get Weller Sooner with the Power of Positive Expectation

"High expectations are the key to everything."
Sam Walton

"There is abundant reason to believe that optimism is useful to a person because positive expectations can be self-fulfilling."
Christopher Peterson, psychologist:

I realize that the following words will probably strike you as a bit tired and overused, but my hope is that by the time you reach the end of this chapter, you will embrace them with all your heart:

We don't get what we want in life; we get what we expect.

Overused or not, you have to admit, those words contain a great deal of wisdom. In fact, more often than not, our expectations turn out to be quite prophetic, don't they? Deep down, most people know this; our lives are a testament to this truth:

- A young boy goes to bat in a Little League baseball game and, as usual, he expects to strike out. He even proclaims this to himself and everyone else. And what usually happens? *"Strike three! You-u-u're out!"*

- A woman heads down the corridor toward her boss' office to ask for a raise, all the while expecting to be turned down. This negative assumption kills her confidence, clouds her face, puts her on the defensive, darkens her voice tone, and negatively affects a hundred and one other subtle cues she unconsciously gives off. And what usually happens? Just as she thought: no St. Thomas getaway this year.

- A boy asks a girl out, all the while expecting to be turned down. His head-full of doubt powers down his mojo and renders him awkward, unsteady, and unconfident. And what does he get? Another Friday night of Snapchat alone.

- Your Aunt Sally is at it again: dooming and glooming about which ailment will attack her next—expecting aches, pains, and illness at every turn. And what do you find cluttering up her calendar? Doctor appointments galore, of course.

- A man gets out of bed and stubs his toe. Five minutes later, he cuts himself shaving. Next, he heads to the kitchen and discovers he's out of coffee pods. He quickly decides that today is going to suck. And voila! He gets that bad day, just as he predicted.

We don't get what we want in life; we get what we expect.

Not a foolproof system perhaps, but a pretty darned consistent one. One would think that, since low expectations have such a dismal track record, people would steer clear of them as much as possible, thus avoiding the unpleasant results that typically follow.

All too often, we don't. And we just keep racking up those dismal outcomes.

Of course, the opposite is every bit as true:

- We fully expect to nail an upcoming presentation at work. The resulting optimism and self-confidence help to put a good dose of zing into our performance. And what do we get? Accolades galore.

- We wake up, smile, take a deep breath, and decide that this day is going to be great. And, no surprise, we have ourselves one heck of a great day.

- We arrive at a party, expecting to have a good time. This puts an engaging smile on our face and warm, charismatic energy in our being. And, miracle of miracles, we do.

- We expect to do well on an upcoming test. Naturally, we then do everything in our power to live up to our high expectations. And what usually happens? Another great test—and more fuel for our future forecasts of success.

- We decide to try an experiment and see if maybe there is something to this "expect a miracle" catchphrase we keep hearing about. So, we start expecting good in all we do. A week later, we decide to keep doing it because we can't help noticing that these past seven days have been curiously and amazingly good.

Yes, we know this, too. The expectation of good stuff to come our way has an almost other-worldly power to become a self-fulfilling prophecy and bring us more of that good stuff.

Which begs the question: If having high or positive expectations so often helps to bring about positive outcomes, why do so many people waste time expecting the worst—and, in so doing, help to bring it about?

It's because of all the naysayers out there, those who go around warning everyone to keep their expectations low (or, as they like to put it: "realistic"). Disappointment, they claim, and even despair, arise when people set their hopes and expectations too high. Better to set them low ("realistic") so as not to be disappointed when things don't turn out the way we would like.

Sure, it makes perfect sense to try to avoid disappointment in life. If only low ("realistic") expectations didn't have such a negative side-effect of their own.

Here's a better approach:

First, when dealing with matters over which you have little or no control—the weather, rude drivers, finding a nonstop flight online, and so on—keep your expectations cautiously optimistic, but know that disappointments will happen sometimes. That's life. We can't avoid every disappointment, no matter how hard we try.

Next, understand that having lofty expectations may not *always* give you everything you want, but, for God's sake, they certainly are not the *cause* of unpleasant outcomes! Expecting the best is enormously better than expecting the worst (or nothing at all). Expecting the best will not jeopardize the outcome. On the contrary, it often helps to improve it.

Finally—and this is important: It is a whole other thing to have high or positive expectations when it concerns matters over which you do have control, especially those involving *your own body*. Since your thinking creates the conditions within your body, your thoughts—including your expectations—are enormously powerful. You *do* have control over your own being, so expecting the best in these matters is a whole different thing and of an entirely different order of power.

Positive expectation is much more effective in matters concerning your own body—over which you have tremendous control.

In addition, positive expectations concerning your own body are even more powerful:

1. When you expect positive outcomes with *full conviction*. We're not talking wishful thinking here, nor lukewarm hope. We're talking full-on, unmitigated conviction.

2. When you call upon the power of positive expectation to power up the eleven other healing strategies presented in this book.

3. When you understand that, although you might not necessarily get the miracle you are expecting, you will, in all likelihood, receive the blessing of an *improved outcome*. So, you expect the best at every turn and wind up with a great deal of improved and often marvelous outcomes for yourself.

Positive expectations may not get you everything you expect in regards to your recovery, but they will very likely help you get more of what you want.

The well-known "Law of Attraction" is operating in full force here. The Law of Attraction, as defined by successconsciousness.com, is:

"The attractive, magnetic power of the Universe that draws similar energies together. It manifests through the power of creation, everywhere and in many ways. This law attracts thoughts, ideas, people, situations, and circumstances."

So, for example, when you send thought-energies of strength and healing out into the Universe and into your own body, they will attract healing energies of a matching frequency to you. We attract that which we focus our thoughts upon. We attract that which we continually *expect*.

And don't forget: The Law of Attraction *is* a Universal *law*. It may only have become known and utilized by the average person for a decade or so (most notably thanks to Rhonda Byrnes' film *The Secret*), but the fact is it has been understood and taken full advantage of by a small handful of enlightened individuals for centuries.

And nowadays, many noted individuals, from Oprah Winfrey to Arnold Schwarzenegger to Steve Harvey, understand and apply the principles of the Law of Attraction to their own lives.

We attract that which we continually expect.

So, in all matters surrounding your body, expect the best, and you will get more of it:

- *Expect your upcoming medical procedure to turn out well.* Frequently imagine a very successful outcome. Think positively about it. Speak positively about it to others. Feel the energy of your positive expectations as they spread throughout your body.

- *Expect your surgery to go well.* Don't expect the worst. Expect the best. And don't merely hope for the best. Expect it! Anticipate a speedy recovery. Expect the pain to be minimal. Expect no complications to arise.

- *Expect your medications to be completely effective.* It matters not in the least whether this expectation produces nothing but a placebo effect rather than a "real" outcome since, when you think about it, the placebo effect *is* a real outcome!

- *Expect good in all things.* The doctors, nurses, and hospital staff will be nice to you. You will be up and walking in only two days, rather than the expected three. You will have less nausea than was predicted. You will keep up your appetite better than expected. You won't lose your hair, as you were told you probably would.

- *After you are well again, continue to expect health and wellness.* Don't go around forecasting when the next medical calamity will strike, or when your "luck will change," or when "the other shoe will drop." Just continue to expect the best from your body right up until the day comes when you have no earthly body to concern yourself with.

Again, you may not get everything you expect, to the full extent that you expect it, but you'll still get *more* of it. You may not get the amazing outcome you're expecting, but you'll still get an *improved* outcome.

And that is the whole point. By expecting the best, you will generally get one of two results:

1. You *will* get the best.

2. You will get at least some measure of improvement.

Either way, you come out ahead.

And there is one more thing you can do to significantly ramp up the potency of positive expectation:

Visualization.

When it comes to bringing about desired improvements in your physiology, visualization truly is the big tamale. If you intend to direct the energy of positive expectation into your body, why not turbocharge the effect with the unparalleled thought-power of your imagination?

The basic practice of visualization is to close your eyes and imagine, over and over, a very positive outcome to your illness or surgery. You mentally "rehearse" this outcome. You repeatedly direct these 3-D healing energies directly to that part of your body that needs them the most.

You see your illness fading away. You see your incision healing perfectly. You see your body growing strong and healthy once again.

But that is just the beginning! Follow the steps below, and you will be giving your body the most potent dose of healing energy it could ever have.

At least twice a day:

1. Get comfortable (or as "comfortable" as you can manage). Close your eyes. Take several deep, long, calming breaths. Just breathe, relax, and clear your mind. Picture only your breath as it moves in...then out.

2. Now, imagine a beam of pure, white, healing light streaming down from the heavens to envelop you and then flow inside your body. Picture it infusing every cell with its powerful healing energy. See the cells of your body cleansed by this energy, strengthened by this energy, healed by this energy, made anew by this energy. Now, direct that beam right to the very part of you that needs it most and repeat the procedure.

3. Practice making your mental movie sharp, detailed, and full of positive

emotion. Make the colors bright, bold, beautiful, and intense. Feel joy, gratitude, warmth, and serenity throughout the process.

4. Feel that healing energy as well. Feel it deeply. Feel its warmth. Feel its ability to soothe. Feel its power. Using your imagination, feel the cells of your body tingling with this energy, healing with this energy, strengthening with this energy.

5. *If you are ill:* Imagine the cells of your immune system (your white blood cells) attacking and killing every diseased cell in your body. Picture these white blood cells as little Pack-men devouring the diseased cells by the millions. Or, picture them as powerful soldiers laying waste to their smaller, weaker enemy (the diseased cells).

If you are recovering from surgery: Visualize and feel every cell in your body being ridden of pain by the white light. Savor the warm, tingling sensation as it moves in to replace the pain with comfort. Conjure up a mental image of the pain being banished from your being. Visualize your incisions healing perfectly and your strength returning. Visualize yourself as healthy and whole.

6. Now take your mental movie and see it play out upon every cell of your body. Imagine each cell as a tiny movie screen showing the same scene of healing at the exact same time. Imagine those trillions of cells playing the same movie of your successful healing process much like when you walk into an electronics store and see fifty TVs playing the same show at the same time. Except, of course, now it's tens of trillions, not fifty.

7. Now, starting with your toes, bring your awareness to each part of your body. "Feel" each part in turn. Then, picture and feel strength, wellness, vitality, healing, and love flooding into every organ, every bone, every muscle, every gland, every tissue, and every membrane. Feel the sensations. No part of your body is left untouched by these energies.

8. Feel the outcome of all these "infusions" throughout your body. Feel the vibration of health and wellness all over. Regardless of how weak or uncomfortable you

may feel at the moment. Imagine how you *will* feel, emotionally and physically, to be well again. Remember, the key to success is to picture your body not the way it *is*, but the way you *want it to be*.

9. Finally, take a few more deep breaths, smile, and feel gratitude for the experience of healing you have just experienced. The Universe gives us more of that for which we are grateful, don't forget.

Positive visualization is virtually unstoppable. Call upon it often.

You don't get what you want in life; you get what you expect. While you are in the hospital or some other medical facility, it behooves you to expect the best in all situations:

- Expect the best from your surgery, your doctors, and your nurses.

- Expect the best from your treatments, your infusions, and your medicines.

- Expect the best from your body and its ability to heal itself.

- Expect the best from the Universe, including its ability to make you well. Feel free to replace the word Universe with Divine Spirit, God, Allah, or whatever term you choose.

- Expect the best from this book. And, while we're on the subject, understand that every one of the twelve strategies presented here will, to a great extent, work as well as you *expect* them to.

- Don't forget to make positive visualization your much-looked-forward-to, twice-a-day ritual from now on until you are well again.

When it comes to your healing, you don't get what you want; you get what you expect.

When it comes to your healing, your positive expectations are king. From this moment forward, make it a habit to expect miracles—especially those that stem from the miracle of your own body.

Affirm the Healing Power of Positive Expectation

Read the following affirmations, silently or aloud, *with conviction and feeling.*

1

I understand that to expect pain or illness increases its likelihood and that to expect wellness increases its likelihood. I expect wellness always.

2

When it comes to my body's health and wellness, I always expect the best and, in so doing, I usually get it.

3

I firmly believe in the power of positive expectation, particularly in matters pertaining to my own body, over which I have enormous control.

4

I expect nothing but the best from my doctors, my nurses, my clinicians, my procedures, my medications, and my own body.

5

I expect to become healthy and to remain healthy. I believe it to my core. Yes, I may nonetheless be stricken with illness on rare occasion, but these occurrences will become far less frequent through my expectations of continued good health.

6

I expect to become healthy and to remain healthy. I believe it to my core. Yes, I may nonetheless be stricken with illness on rare occasion, but my recovery from these illnesses will be accelerated by my positive expectations.

7

If and when I have an illness, I completely, confidently, and continually expect a smooth and speedy recovery—just as I am doing right now.

8

I expect, with conviction, that whatever pain or illness I have will be mild and short-lived.

9

I wholeheartedly believe in the power and efficacy of any medications given to me. I understand that these medicines will generally work as well as I expect them to.

10

I understand that, if placebos have the power to heal, then certainly a real drug can and will do the same for me and more. I fully expect that all my medications will work exactly as promised—or better.

11

I fully expect my body's powerful immune system to seek out and destroy any and all diseases that come my way.

12

I know that my thinking creates my body. Therefore, I call upon the power of my mind to visualize rapid healing within my body.

13

When I am ill or recovering from surgery, I spend my free time visualizing being well. I *imagine* how good it will feel to be back on my feet. I *feel* how good it will feel to be back to my old self again.

14

When I am ill, I spend my free tine visualizing my body's immune system killing every diseased cell in my body.

15

I expect to heal quickly from my illness. I see myself healing quickly. I feel myself healing quickly.

16

I *expect* a rapid recovery from surgery. I *see* myself recovering quickly. I *feel* myself recovering quickly.

17

I may not always get everything I expect, but I understand that my positive expectations will generally improve my overall condition and accelerate my healing.

18

When I am ill, I spend part of my free time conjuring up mini mental movies of my body's unstoppable immune system attacking and destroying every diseased cell I have.

19

I don't anticipate problems or complications during my recovery. There is nothing to be gained by my being "realistic."

20

I understand that nothing negative will ever result from my positive expectations. But plenty of good can and will come from them.

21

I visualize wellness, healing, and successful outcomes in all matters concerning my medical condition.

22

I have no use for any expectations that may harm or weaken my body's ability to heal. I keep my expectations one hundred percent positive.

23

I practice "inverse paranoia" by continually expecting everything to go well for me and work out for my benefit and, in so doing, make these outcomes more likely.

24

I fully understand that my expectation of a rapid and smooth recovery from illness or surgery is one of the greatest medicines on Earth.

25

I accept, acknowledge, believe in, and embrace the proven power of positive expectation to aid in my healing process.

Healing Actions

Here are three things you can do, starting today, to help you more fully utilize the incredible healing power of positive expectation:

1. Expect to get better

No matter what, always maintain a well-practiced, positive conviction that you *will* heal or recover from whatever medical setback comes your way, that you will do so quickly, and that you will do so in a manner better than expected.

2. Expect things to go well

Tests, procedures, surgeries, infusions, consultations, treatments—begin right now to make a habit of always expecting a positive outcome from all your experiences in the hospital or treatment center. You may not always get everything you want, but by maintaining an unwavering practice of expecting the best, you will most assuredly *increase* the likelihood of a successful outcome and help to improve the outcome itself.

3. Expect miracles

If you've not yet done so, join the ranks of the many who have begun to act upon the popular catch-phrase: "Expect miracles." You have nothing to lose and everything to gain by expecting miracles throughout your hospital stay and beyond.

4

Get Weller Sooner with the Power of Your Inner Strength

"Nothing can dim the light which shines from within."

Maya Angelou

"You never know how strong you are until being strong is the only choice you have."

Bob Marley

Here is the next item to add to your healing and recovery toolkit:

Your own God-given inner strength.

If you are ill, you must choose to remain strong—strong-willed and strong minded—and, in so doing, return strength to your physical body. Never regard your illness or condition as being larger or more powerful than you. Never allow it to have the upper hand. Be confident, be strong, and never stop seeing yourself as the ultimate victor.

Through all phases of surgery: from pre-op jitters to post-op pain and nausea—and through all facets of illness, from pain and weakness to fear and depression—you *must* remain strong. You must call upon your inner strength to fight what may turn out to be a long battle against the ravages of your surgery or disease.

- You must keep your body strong by eating the best food you can get and by eating even when you don't feel like it (unless you are instructed not to eat by your doctor, or are simply too nauseous to keep anything down).

- You must keep your muscles strong by moving in whatever capacity you can. Even curling and uncurling your fingers, toes, and biceps is better than nothing— far better. Even simple isometrics— repeatedly tightening and relaxing various muscles—can be a great help. Tighten, hold for a count of four, release for a count of four. Repeat.

- You must keep the cells, tissues, and organs of your body, as well as your immune system, strong enough to defeat any viral, bacterial, or other intruders by continually regarding your entire body, inside and out, as strong and resilient.

- You must keep your mind and your spirit strong and not allow yourself to succumb to any negative mental or emotional energy brought to you from within or without, that is to say from your own negative ruminations or those of others.

Yes, you must remain strong for the duration. This is imperative. I'll even go so far as to implore you to remain strong, tough, and unbeatable!

But how, you may be wondering. How do I do that? Where is this amazing "inner strength" going to come from—especially at a time when my body is weakened by my illness or surgery?

Answer: Your inner strength comes to you simply by your *choosing* to be strong. It comes to you via your *will* to be strong.

Furthermore, it comes to you by your decision to *act* strong, to conduct yourself from a place of strength, and even to speak in the way of an individual filled with inner strength.

Behavior is the genesis of feeling. Act strong, and you will become strong.

Yes, it really is that simple. You see, you already have all the inner strength that you need to do whatever must be done to ensure your victory against whatever medical adversity you may be facing. It is already inside you—all you need to do is summon it!

Your inner strength is already inside you. It comes to you simply by your choosing to be strong.

That's how it works with this kind of strength. You get it by simply calling upon it— by choosing to utilize it. Remember, we're not talking about muscular strength or strength in the athletic sense. Lifting weights, running marathons, and the like are achieved by building strength through _training_.

But in regards to strength that emanates from within—from your mind, your will, or your spirit—this is not the case. You simply choose it. You simply and assertively decide that you have it and that you will use it. You acknowledge and affirm that you already have inner strength— that you've found it within yourself before and can find it again.

Then you call upon it.
Then you utilize it.

- You are stronger than your illness—if you choose to be.

- You can find the strength within you to ride out periods of pain, weakness, or nausea—if you choose to do so.

- You can find the power within yourself to fight and to keep on fighting for as long as it takes—if you decide to do so.

- You can muster emotional strength to help you overcome waves of fear, worry, uncertainty, and depression that may come your way—if you so desire.

- You can be tough—tougher than whatever situation you may find yourself in—if you want to be, and for as long as you need to be.

Any form of inner strength you need is yours simply by deciding that you already have it.

Whatever you need—whatever form of inner strength you need: fortitude, tenacity, determination, grit, mettle, moxie, nerve, pluck, spunk, staying power, backbone, gutsiness, intrepidity, spine, or willpower will come to you if you simply decide, and repeatedly affirm, that you already have it.

I should add that the summoning of inner strength is not purely a matter of willpower or force. It is also a matter of the mind-body connection we discussed in the first chapter. Your body is *made* by your thinking. It is made healthy by your thinking.

And it is made *strong* by your thinking.

You see, feeling strong on the level of thought and feeling is great, and you will benefit greatly from the boost of confidence, conviction, and tenacity it will give you. But this is only where it starts. These thoughts and feelings of strength will also manifest in your body on a *physical* level—on a material level, so to speak. In other words, thinking strength and feeling strength—continually and with conviction—will also result in the "toughening up" of your physical being.

However, we need to make an important distinction here. Thinking "strength" does not mean that you become magically strong in an athletic sense. You can't assume that by merely thinking "strength," you will suddenly be able to bench-press two hundred pounds or run a mile in five minutes. These types of capabilities still require training, as they always have.

What it does mean is that, by calling upon your inner strength through your thoughts, words, and chosen feelings of strength, you provide your body with more of the physical fortitude and toughness you need to help you weather any illness, cope better with pain, and power through periods of nausea, fatigue, lethargy, or weakness. This includes your body's ability to fight illness and infection, to mend itself, and to steel itself against whatever physiological hardship that may come your way.

Think about it: We've all known or heard about certain individuals who just seem to muscle through illness or recover from surgery more robustly than most people. And we want to be like them. Now, maybe these people have had a history of moving through life with a good supply of grit, fortitude, and tenacity, so their ability to sail through medical setbacks is, to them, par for the course.

But their inner strength was nonetheless borne of nothing more than choice, even if these choices were made subconsciously at some earlier point in their lives.

And so it will be with you. The more you remind yourself that you are strong on the inside, where it counts, the more strength you will find at your disposal—both the psychological and the physiological kinds.

Sure, you will probably feel too tired or demoralized to act with strength sometimes. But this is precisely when you need to be strong the most. Do not allow thoughts of giving up or defeat to take up residence anywhere inside you. Fight and fight some more!

And let us not forget the first cousin of inner strength:

Courage.

You also must maintain a feeling of courage against whatever medical challenges or setbacks you may face. And, once again, remember that courage, too, is yours for the using by nothing more than your *decision* to exercise it.

You may have doubts here. You may feel that you can't stop yourself from feeling fear while you are ill or facing a difficult surgery and recovery process.

But that is not the point.

Having courage doesn't mean that you feel no fear. It doesn't mean that you don't get scared. The definition of courage is: acting *with* fear; it does not suggest the absence of fear. It means that you feel fear, you acknowledge that you are afraid, and then you act anyway. It means that you do anything that must be done during your illness or before and after your surgery, even while you are feeling the fear.

Courage is acting with fear; it is not the absence of fear.

But remember: Even if you have every right and every reason to feel fear at this time, that does not mean that you have to give the fear more power and dominion over yourself by fixating on it. Don't give strength to your fear by telling yourself over and over that you have "every right" to feel afraid. Perhaps you do have the right. But is exercising this "right" in your emotional or physiological best interest?

Not on your life.

So, acknowledge the fear and accept the fear. Say, "Yep, I'm feeling scared right now." Then, set these thoughts aside and get right back in there and fight! Get right back in there and start focusing once again on more productive tasks such as building your strength, bolstering your positivity, practicing your positive visualization, and sending good, strong, positive, and courageous energies into the cells of your body.

Because, don't forget, whenever you send thoughts of strength and courage into your body, you are *building* a body that is strong and courageous. You are *creating* a tougher, more unbeatable physiology that will help you in your healing or recovery process.

One more thing: As an adjunct to your being strong and courageous, I suggest that you go the extra mile by remaining *unbuggable* as well.

Back in the late 1980s, studies were conducted involving centenarians (people with lifespans of one hundred years or more). Researchers wanted to determine which life-style traits were the most prevalent among these individuals. They looked at such life compo-nents as diet, exercise, work, spirituality, and so on. And the top trait among the world's oldest citizens was that they are, in a word, *unbuggable*. They are very good at not caving in even under the most trying of circumstances, rolling with the punches life throws at them, remaining level-headed and at peace, and remaining positive and optimistic through it all.

You are advised to do the same.

Be unbuggable. Don't let this illness or surgery get to you.

Remind yourself over and over: "Be unbuggable. Be unbuggable." Do your best not to let your illness, fear, or pain get to you. Be unbuggable as a means of strengthening your mind, body, spirit, and immune system against whatever medical misadventures you may face. Just keep your cool, maintain equanimity (mental calmness), and transcend any challenges that come your way with self-assuredness and grace.

And this, too, of course, is a matter of *choice*. Remaining unbuggable is something you acquire by your simple decision to do so, along with your willingness to exercise this empowering lifestyle practice.

There you have it. Be strong. Be tough. Be brave. Be unbuggable. With these chosen traits, you can remain unfazed and unbeaten by even the toughest medical displeasures you may face, now and in the future.

Affirm the Healing Power of Your Inner Strength

Read the following affirmations, silently or aloud, *with conviction and feeling*.

1

I am stronger than my illness.

2

I am tougher than my pain.

3

I am more powerful than the diseased cells taking up temporary residence inside me. Like healthy cells, diseased cells are *my* cells. They belong to me, and they are every bit under my control as every other cell in my body.

4

I am strong, tough, and resilient in the face of any medical challenge that comes my way.

5

I am more persistent than my illness.

6

I choose to remain mentally strong, emotionally resilient, and physically tough.

7

I choose to call upon my vast reserves of inner strength in fighting this illness.

8

Acting from strength or weakness is always my choice. I choose to act from strength.

9

I've got a whole lot of fight inside me!

10

My body's immune system is ultimately more powerful than my illness.

11

My immune system can easily kill any unwelcome germs, bacteria, or cells that temporarily invade my body.

12

My immune system is powerful, unbeatable, and very good at what it does.

13

My spirit is unshakable and unbreakable.

14

My body is tough—if I say it is.

15

My soul is resilient—if I say it is.

16

My immune system is unbeatable—if I say it is.

17

When I am ill, I think thoughts of strength, power, tenacity, grit, and ultimate victory.

18

I don't give in, and I don't give up.

19

I intend to give this fight everything I have— and I expect nothing short of victory.

20

I choose to call upon all the inner strength I can muster in fighting my illness or bolstering my healing after surgery—and to reap all the rewards of accelerated recovery.

21

I have all the fortitude, tenacity, grit, determination, mettle, moxie, nerve, pluck, staying power, backbone, gutsiness, spine, intrepidity, and willpower I will ever need.

22

I am one tough cookie when I need to be, and when I choose to be.

23

I have courage. No matter how afraid I may feel right now, I face things head on, and I do whatever needs doing and face whatever needs facing.

24

I am unbuggable. I choose not to let this situation get to me. I keep my cool and roll with whatever comes along.

25

I accept, acknowledge, believe in, and
embrace the power of my inner strength to
aid in the healing process.

Healing Actions

Here are three things you can do, starting today, to help you summon your vast reserve of inner strength:

1. Think strong

Remind yourself, over and over, that inner strength resides in all of us, and it is simply one choice away. Repeat often: "I have the strength I need to heal quickly and completely.". Know the truth: that inner strength, courage, and an unbuggable nature are traits we all can call upon and utilize at will.

2. Speak strong

Use strong, confident, positive language when speaking with others about your medical condition. Use words of strength such as: *will, can, do, win, succeed,* and *yes.* And don't forget to keep your voice strong and powerful as well— no playing the "victim" role.

3. Act strong

As the saying goes: "Act as if and you shall become." Face your illness, surgery, or recovery with the attitude and spirit of a victor, not a victim. If you are offered any opportunity to walk, carry yourself as strongly and erectly as you can. Walk and move in the surest, most confident way possible. This is not an all-or-nothing venture, however. If you feel too weak or uncomfortable to do anything more than just holding your head higher or speaking with a stronger voice, that is perfectly fine. It all helps.

5

Get Weller Sooner by Becoming the Perfect Patient

"Never walk into a hospital crying. Have an attitude that you will make someone else's life better."
Jim Kelly, NFL quarterback

"Your karma should be good, and everything else will follow. Your good karma will always win over your bad luck."
Rohit Shetty, Indian film producer/director

Making the decision, right here and now, to be the perfect patient will have a powerful and positive effect on your ability to get weller sooner in two different yet interconnected ways.

106

First, consider these two extremes:

On one side of the corridor, we have a patient who somehow feels entitled to be mean-spirited, demanding, and rude with doctors, nurses, hospital staff, other patients, and even family members. He's scared and in pain, so he drops his normally pleasant demeanor and starts lashing out at anyone and everyone.

He becomes difficult. He speaks in less-than-amiable tones, often playing the angry victim role. He'll moan, groan, criticize, blame, and complain. He's uncooperative when it comes to any aspect of his treatment that he doesn't like. He'll resist taking his medications. He'll refuse to get up and walk around when told to do so. He complains about the food. He'll wear a sour or dour face throughout the day. He'll bitch and whine and ultimately wind up being the primary cause of his having a rotten time while in the hospital (rottener than it might have been anyway).

And when I say "having a rotten time," I mean that in a physical or medical sense as well—as you will see.

I often wonder: Do people like that truly think that their grouchiness or mean-spirited-ness is somehow good for their disease-battered or surgery-battered body? Since when were any of these traits beneficial to anyone's health, let alone their happiness?

Furthermore, since they often aren't doing exactly what they're told in regards to, say, exercise or nutrition (that is, taking good care of themselves), their healing is very likely compromised or delayed even further.

And that is the choice they make. The problem is, as I said, it doesn't do them a bit of good.

On the other side of the corridor, we find a patient who chooses instead to be polite, appreciative, understanding, cooperative, accepting, gracious, and good-natured *even if or when* she feels poorly or her care is lacking in some way.

- She chooses to make the best of her situation, no matter what the situation may be. Notice I said, "*chooses.*"

- She chooses to do exactly as she is told: She eats as she is advised and takes her medications willingly. She walks and does physical therapy as instructed. She follows all instructions from her doctors to the letter—*because, after all, it's for* her *benefit.*

- She's friendly, polite, and understanding. She smiles when being administered to or spoken to—at least as much as her condition allows (don't forget what I said in Chapter 2 about the benefits of smiling).

- She gladly and appreciatively takes advantage of any resources made available to her, from informative literature, to support groups, to nutrition counseling—*again, because it is for her benefit.*

Her friendly, cooperative behavior goes a long way in helping to accelerate her recovery. And, in the end, it boosts her spirits as well by making her feel good about herself.

Certainly, patients are in a more positive mental and emotional state when they're pleasant to everyone. And their positive demeanor and behavior send powerfully positive energies into their bodies, helping further to speed the healing process.

Sound too good to be true? Trust me; these people are out there. But you have to look carefully; they're harder to spot because they generally are not the ones making noise or creating a scene.

Now, perhaps you're somewhere in the middle between those two extremes. Nonetheless, you, too, will benefit tremendously when you shift yourself even closer to the perfect patient camp.

> *Your positive demeanor and behavior send powerfully positive energy into your body, helping to speed the healing process.*

So, behaving as the perfect patient gives you more opportunities for positive self-care and healing. And that makes your body feel good. Furthermore, it makes your spirit feel good, which, in turn, sends more positive energies into your body, making your body feel even better. Beautiful upward spiral, wouldn't you say?

Second, there is the matter of *karma.*

Karma can be defined this way: In life, you get what you give. It's a form of "cause and effect." What goes around comes around. You reap what you sow. So, if you're nice, you get "nice" back, in some form or other. If you are unpleasant toward others, you get "unpleasant" back, again, in one form or another.

Karma is an ancient Eastern practice that has been around for centuries. It isn't infallible, of course. Yes, sometimes bad things do happen to good people, and vice-versa. But *in general,* it is a remarkably reliable equation by which to steer your life.

Now, when you behave positively or negatively toward, say, a particular nurse, the positive or negative that goes around and comes back around to you may not necessarily be from that same person. It's seldom a matter of that same nurse saying, "Well, since she was rude to me, maybe I'll just take my sweet time in getting her ginger ale." Mostly what is going on is simply your negative energy bringing back more of the same to you—in whatever form the Universe might deem right and just for you.

Say you're behaving in an inconsiderate manner. Then, over the course of the day, that inconsiderateness is returned to you, perhaps in the form of an inconsiderate roommate blaring the TV, or an MRI that winds up being fraught with problems and delays.

Negative out, negative back—one way or another.

On the other hand, say you assume the demeanor and behavior of the perfect patient— the polite, easygoing, positive individual who just seems to brighten the day of everyone around her. This positive energy may return to you in the form of more visits from friends and family, or blood work numbers that come back better than expected, or members of your medical team being just a touch more attentive to you.

Positive out, positive back—one way or another.

As Wikipedia puts it: "Good intent and good deeds contribute to good karma and future happiness."

Let's make that: "future happiness and *healing*."

> *The positive energy you give to others will come back to you. In some way or other, it will result in an improved healing process for you.*

So, if you are a patient who is polite, friendly, easygoing, and cooperative to every doctor, nurse, technician, staff member, and fellow patient you come in contact with, then:

You'll feel better *emotionally*. It feels good to do good and to be good. Your spirit will be lifted. You'll have a brighter, more positive outlook. You'll get "friendly" back from others, perhaps not from everyone, but certainly, more than the grouch down the hall is going to get. And this will make you happier, too.

You'll feel better *physically*. Here's that mind-body connection again. Your positive behavior and positive interactions will boost your thoughts and emotions. These, in turn, will convey positive, healing energy to your body.

Furthermore, those people working on your behalf may treat you with more kindness and compassion and be more willing to work harder and in a more caring manner with the patient who is doing their best to be gracious. Sure, these people are professionals, so they'll most likely act kindly toward you regardless of whether or not you return the gesture. But, come on, you know perfectly well which sort of patient is more likely to get members of their medical team going the extra mile for them.

Sure, sometimes you have to stand up for yourself and complain about some "infraction" regarding your care. But consider your own bedside manner while doing so. You can point out these sorts of things without being hurtful or accusatory. Yes, you have the "right" to be less than congenial, but, again, is that going to make you feel better or heal faster in the end?

When I pay a visit to a recovery ward or perhaps a chemotherapy infusion center, I'm amazed to take in the vast range of behaviors among the patients. Frankly, it's often night and day.

On one side of the room, I'll see patients who are bitter, rude, or rundown looking. On the other side of the room, I'll see patients who are polite, positive, well-dressed, well-groomed, and strong. And in both cases, it is their *choices* that bring about these behaviors.

But here's the amazing part: When you closely watch someone putting out good karma, you come to realize that it isn't one iota harder to be the courteous, pleasant, positive patient than to be the grumbling, complaining, negative one.

It's mostly just a matter of making the *choice* that brightens everyone's day—yours included.

Seriously, when it comes to matters of healing and recovery, rest assured that karma is hard at work—for you or against you—your choice.

So, putting this all together, acting as the perfect patient:

1. Speeds and improves your recovery in the *physical realm*. You're taking advantage of every positive resource you can, from eating right, taking your medications correctly, getting the right amount of rest and exercise, and so on. You're helping your body by doing the right things for your body and to your body.

2. Speeds and improves your recovery in the *mind-body sense*. Your cheerfulness and positive demeanor send positive, healing energies directly into your body, enhancing its self-healing mechanisms, making it stronger and healthier.

3. Speeds and improves your recovery in the *interpersonal dimension*. Being the patient who doctors, nurses, and other hospital staff members want to be around and do their best for helps to ensure that you receive the very best care you possibly can.

4. Speeds and improves your recovery in the *karmic sense*. You get what you give. When you give your best to everyone, the Universe will see to it that you will get back more of what you give out—one way or another, in one form or another.

Acting as the perfect patient is a win-win for everyone. It makes you feel better emotionally, spiritually, and physically. It makes the people around you feel good. It puts you in more direct contact with all the good that the Universe can give.

And acting as the perfect patient is, again, every bit as easy as not doing so. Smiling is easy.

Friendly is easy. Kindness is easy. Cooperative is easy. And each one is nothing more than a decision away. Frankly, anger and the like use up more energy and wear you out more than anything else!

Behaving as the perfect patient requires little more than your simple decision to do so.

Finally, if you want to amplify the effects of good karma, don't forget that the power of positive expectation factors in here as well. *Believe* in the power of good karma. *Expect* to get back that which you give out. *Know* that karma is real, and it is powerful. *Embrace* the spirit of putting out good karma with a sincere and loving heart.

Do these, become the perfect patient, and watch the magic unfold.

Affirm Your Role as the Perfect Patient

Read the following affirmations, silently or aloud, *with conviction and feeling.*

1

Whenever I am sick or recovering from surgery, I choose to behave as the perfect patient—for the good of all, including myself.

2

I do exactly as I am told by my doctors and nurses, and I do so with positivity and kindness.

3

Every day, I choose to act as the perfect patient, one who is respected and well-liked by everyone working on my behalf, one who is everyone's favorite.

4

I'm well aware that my positive behavior and outlook take no more energy than their opposites.

5

I intend to give off good karma for the duration of my hospitalization; my body will respond with improved healing.

6

I offer smiles to everyone I meet. It makes me happy. It makes others happy. It aids in my healing process.

7

My cooperative spirit sends powerful healing energy throughout my body.

8

I do exactly as I am told by my medical team with the understanding and the conviction that it will speed my recovery.

9

To the best of my ability, I am pleasant, polite, and kind to my caregivers. I understand karma; I understand that what goes around, comes around.

10

I am grateful to my doctors and nurses, and I show it through my kind words, pleasant demeanor, and positive energy.

11

I choose to send out loving energy to everyone on my medical team, for it will return in kind.

12

My smiles, positive disposition, and kind words are an inspiration to other patients.

13

I enfold myself in a healing aura of positivity and goodwill, which inspires the members of my medical team.

14

My body is healed every bit as much by the positive energy that I direct outward as that which I direct inward.

15

My choosing to behave as the perfect patient benefits everyone with whom I come in contact, including myself.

16

I understand that the energy I give out is returned to me in kind by the Universe.

17

If I have to be in this hospital for a while, I intend to make it as positive an experience as I possibly can—and I know that my body will thank me later.

18

Being the perfect patient provides just as much benefit to my physical health and well-being as it does to my spirit.

19

I'm well aware that my acting as the perfect patient is no more difficult than not acting this way.

20

To the best of my ability, I greet everyone who comes into my room with kind words and a smile.

21

I don't use my hospitalization as an excuse to put out negative energy of any kind. I choose instead to make the best of my situation and to do so with a kind heart.

22

I have no use for sullen, forlorn, gloomy, impatient, impolite, or any other such behavior. In the end, it does no one, including myself, a bit of good. For the benefit of my mind, body, and spirit, I am all about contentedness, graciousness, appreciativeness, and a positive outlook.

23

I enjoy doing whatever I can to brighten the day of everyone I meet, knowing that it brightens my day as well.

24

My healing and recovery are augmented by my upbeat, appreciative, and warm behavior.

25

I accept, acknowledge, believe in, and embrace the benefits to my healing and recovery process that come from my choosing to behave as the perfect patient along with my sending out good karma to all.

Healing Actions

Here are three things you can do, starting today, to help you become the kind of patient who will be fondly remembered by all who come in contact with you during your hospitalization—and the kind of patient whose body benefits all the more for it:

1. Do what you are told

Take all medications exactly as directed. Move and exercise exactly as you are instructed. Eat as you are advised to eat. Read carefully any literature with which you are provided. Do all these things cheerfully, appreciatively, and with positive expectations.

2. Be a role model for other patients

Speak with kindness and understanding to all other patients with whom you come in contact, no matter how poorly you may be feeling. Remind yourself that it takes no more energy to be kind than to be negative or hostile. Remember that it's not whether you have a "right" to be negative; it's whether or not it is in your *best interest* to be anything but gracious.

3. Be the patient everyone wants to help

Be friendly, polite, appreciative, and cooperative with all doctors, nurses, technicians, and orderlies working on your behalf. Make them want to be in the room with you. Give them the incentive to want to do their best for you and possibly even go the extra mile for you.

6

Get Weller Sooner with the Power of Laughter

"Against the assault of laughter, nothing can stand."
Mark Twain

"I have not seen anyone dying of laughter, but I know millions who are dying because they are not laughing."
Dr. Madan Kataria

Chances are, you're really going to have to open up your mind for this one. Ready? Here it is: Aside from being a whole lot of fun...

Laughter heals. Laughter cures. Literally and profoundly.

Laughter heals. Laughter cures. Literally and profoundly.

Laugh all you want, but when it comes to matters of health and healing, the therapeutic power of laughter is no laughing matter. Frankly, it is nothing short of remarkable. It does *so* much for our physiology that it should be part of everyone's daily regimen, both in the hospital and out. And, rest assured, there are *no* adverse side effects (except perhaps the possibility of disturbing a few stomach staples with your belly laughs).

And, the benefits of laughter in healing are not only remarkable; they are undeniable. It doesn't take long to go online and find study after study and article after article, many penned by respected authorities in the field of medicine, attesting to and outright proving the power of laughter to aid the body in healing.

According to Cancer Treatment Centers of America, humor therapy, as it is known, has been used by doctors and surgeons since as far back as the 13th century. By the late 20th century, scientific studies were being conducted on the effects of laughter on physical wellness. Much of this stemmed from the writing of Norman Cousins, who, in the late 70s, after suffering for years from a painful and debilitating inflammation of the spine, took matters into his own hands and cured himself of his illness using a strict daily regimen of Marx

Brothers movies and episodes of *Candid Camera*. He recounted this remarkable story in his 1979 book: *Anatomy of an Illness.*

Now, consider these words from Allen B. Weisse, M.D., in his article "Humor in Medicine: Can Laughter Help in Healing?" (Baylor University Medical Center):

"In 1982, paleontologist Stephen J. Gould, then 40 years old, was found to have an abdominal mesothelioma, a rare but aggressive cancer with a median survival time of only eight months. Rather than sink into hopelessness and despair, Gould decided to fight with proper attitude lined up with excellent medical management. He survived for twenty years following the diagnosis. Gould wrote about that first battle with cancer in 1985 in a paper entitled 'The Median Isn't the Message.' In it, he concluded that 'The swords of battle are numerous, and none more effective than humor.'"

There is no shortage of individuals like him, claiming and even proving to have cured their "incurable" illnesses using nothing but, or little more than, a continual diet of laughter. Now, perhaps the jury is still out on whether or not there is hard scientific data proving, or at least validating such claims. So, you should in no way interpret my words as in any way suggesting that one might consider trying to heal himself or herself from any disease with laughter alone.

But—and this is a big but—there are reams of credible medical data proving that a daily laughter regimen can and will significantly aid in the efficacy of existing cancer treatments— likewise, for the treatment of just about any illness you care to name. Laughter makes the healing process far more rapid and complete than conventional treatments alone.

No joke. Laughter improves our physiology in many ways. Here are several to consider:

1. Laughter positively affects your muscles and nearby organs. It massages muscles from within and helps them to relax. It gives them a light workout, so to speak.

2. Laughter strengthens and invigorates your immune system. It boosts T-cell activity (cells that help fight against infections, tumors, and other intruders).

3. Laughter increases the release of the "feel-good" brain chemical known as endorphins, which, by the way, are what bring about the intoxicating phenom- enon known as "runner's high."

4. Laughter helps to lower your blood pressure.

5. Laughter helps to decrease your level of pain during illness or following surgery.

6. Laughter even helps to reduce inflammation throughout your body—and inflammation at the cellular level is commonly shown to be the underlying cause of almost every disease or ailment you care to name.

Laughter heals and helps improve your physiology in so many ways.

Bottom line: The evidence suggesting and often proving the power of humor and laughter to aid in healing—and even to create healing—is irrefutable.

But remember, it will work more or less in lockstep with your *belief* in its power to heal and your positive *expectation* of its success.

And if something works, it works! Just embrace it with all your heart, soul, and belly muscles, then reap all the rewards it can give.

I urge you to make laughter part of your healing and recovery regimen. Sure, you're going to do all the other standard practices as well: Getting enough rest and physical activity, taking your medications, getting your infusions, and so on. But, seriously, laughter is every bit as important.

And, to that end, here is the best news of all: Unlike Norman Cousins' having to content himself with the hit-and-miss offering of funny programs and movies on pre-cable television, we have virtually millions of options available to help bring out enough snickers, chortles, and snorts to help rid your body of just about any form of pain or illness you may have. Modern technology and the Internet have made it *so* easy to obtain catalysts for laughter that there isn't even enough time in a lifetime to sample them all. Here are a few possibilities:

- Listen to stand-up comedy on XM radio or Pandora.

- Watch your favorite stand-up comedians on YouTube.

- Stream funny videos, including funny TV shows and movies, right to your phone.

- Get a couple of joke-a-day apps for your phone.

- Search for and then visit comedy and humor web sites. Find items that tickle your funny bone. Laugh yourself silly.

And hold nothing back! No matter how silly or even obnoxious your howling may seem to anyone nearby, just let it all out—laugh deep, long, and loud. Don't forget: Your healing process is more important than what someone else may think in regards to your hysterics.

The Internet has made it easy to obtain all the catalysts for laughter that you could ever want.

And when comedy recordings or broadcasts aren't available, just laugh for no reason. Quietly, if you must (out of respect for your roommate), but laugh just the same. Force it if you have to. Fake it if you must. But just smile, laugh, and keep a great sense of humor about you—even during the most trying periods of your hospital stay as well as your follow-up recuperation at home.

Remember, it is during your most trying periods that you need the health benefits of laughter the most.

Bottom line: Laugh as much as possible and, while you're at it, don't take the situation you're in, or yourself, too seriously—even if it *is* a serious matter. Being down, dark, dour, and depressed will not help your situation in any way. It won't do your mind, body, or spirit a bit of good. If you can't find humor in the situation, invent some. It is your choice where you focus your attention and in which frame of mind you do so.

> *Laughter can come from your own sense of humor every bit as much as it can from a stand-up comic.*

Just lighten up in every way you can. It's for your health and healing and, as such, it really is *no* laughing matter.

LOL.

Affirm the Healing Power of Laughter

Read the following affirmations, silently or aloud, *with conviction and feeling.*

1

I understand and acknowledge the incredible and proven power of laughter to aid my healing and recovery.

2

I'm never too sick or too weak to watch or listen to stand-up comedy routines or funny movies and laugh myself into more rapid healing.

3

I don't need a "reason" to laugh—just a desire to help my body to get weller sooner.

4

I fully believe in the power of laughter, and so my body reaps all the benefits laughter provides.

5

If I say that humor helps me to heal faster, then it helps me to heal faster.

6

I understand that laughter truly is the best medicine; Science has proven time and time again that laughter strengthens my immune system and helps to rid my body of disease.

7

I don't care one bit if anyone thinks I've gone off my rocker because I spend so much time laughing. This is all about healing, not "keeping up appearances."

8

When it comes to healing and getting out of the hospital sooner, I take my sense of humor very seriously.

9

Benefiting from laughter is one of the easiest and most enjoyable ways I know to keep my body in a strong healing mode.

10

I am grateful to have discovered the powerful role that laughter provides me while I'm in the hospital.

11

My smiles, laughter, and sense of humor have the most amazing healing effect on me.

12

I am well aware that life itself is filled with humor. I'm getting better at finding humor in many situations.

13

I don't "edit" my laughter. I don't hold it inside. I don't "tone it down," unless absolutely necessary. When I laugh, I just let go and let it out.

14

I can laugh myself out of any illness to the extent that I believe I can.

15

While in the hospital or at home recuperating, I've made it a habit to fill my phone with joke-a-day apps, humor web sites, Pandora or XM comedy channels, YouTube video playlists of my favorite stand-up comics, and links to any funny old movies or TV shows I can find.

16

Whenever I can't manage to laugh, I can always, at the very least, choose to smile— whether I have a "reason" to smile or not.

17

I've learned to let go completely of any inhibitions I may have that hold me back from fully enjoying many of the amusing moments that make up my day.

18

When I laugh, I visualize its joyful, healing energy spreading throughout my body. I imagine it strengthening me, invigorating me, and shaking loose any diseased cells.

19

When I laugh, I can feel it infuse my body with powerfully positive, healing energy.

20

I know, with deep conviction, that laughter goes a long way in helping me to get strong, get well, and get out of the hospital sooner.

21

I fully understand and believe in the power of laughter to help accelerate my healing.

22

Following the advice of Ralph Waldo Emerson, I make it a point to "laugh often and much."

23

I may not "feel" like laughing right now, but I understand that this is precisely when I need the healing energy of laughter the most.

24

Every time I laugh, I can feel its healing energy coursing through me and helping to make me well.

25

I accept, acknowledge, believe in, and embrace the proven power of laughter to aid in my healing process.

Healing Actions

Here are three things you can do, starting today, to help heal your body with the power of humor.

1. Find laughter on the Internet

From stand-up comedy on YouTube, Pandora, or XM Radio, to funny movies and TV shows, to humor web sites, the Net is awash in laughter. Surf around and find as much laughter-inducing material as you can. Then enjoy it often.

2. Find the humor in it

Life itself offers us many opportunities to tickle our funny-bones—providing that we look for them and allow ourselves the opportunity to laugh at them. Yes, being in the hospital is a serious matter, but so is the use of laughter as an aid in healing.

3. Laugh for no reason

Laughing itself is what it's about, so whether or not you have a good "reason" to laugh, laugh anyway. Silently if you must, out of respect for your roommate, but allow the benefits of laughter to be yours even if it is for no apparent reason at all.

7

Get Weller Sooner with the Power of Music

"Music is therapy. Music moves people. It connects people in ways that no other medium can. It pulls heart strings. It acts as medicine."
Macklemore

"Music has healing power. It has the ability to take people out of themselves for a few hours."
Elton John

Consider this: The Chinese character for medicine includes the character for music. Now, if you know anything about Chinese characters, you know that a) they contain a whole lot of wisdom, and b) they go back a long, long way. Medicine and music—one of the world's oldest,

140

most beautiful, and most powerful partner-ships.

In Greek mythology, Apollo is recognized as the original source of health and healing. Perusing *Cassell's Dictionary of Classical Mythology* by Jenny March, we see:

"Apollo's lyre symbolizes the gift of music, which is the harmony of sounds. To have health and healing, there must be a harmonious order-ing of all the vital forces within the organism; all the strings must be in tune. There's a deep therapeutic relationship between music and healing."

Then there is the matter of Hippocrates, who is said to have treated his patients with music nearly 2500 years ago. There is also the matter of native Americans, who have been doing the very same thing for centuries.

All in all, the healing power of music as an aid in healing has been known and utilized all over the world for millennia.

Pretty impressive track record. And now, modern science is getting in on the act and proving them right. Myriad studies are provid-ing us with irrefutable data on music's incred-ible (not to mention safe, painless, uplifting, virtually free, and easy-to-obtain) power to make us well.

Music has been used to help patients get weller sooner for thousands of years. Today, doctors are continuing this powerful and proven healing tradition.

Once again, I'm going to remind you that your body is made of energy. And music is energy as well—actually, more like a suite of different energies. There is the rhythmic, uplifting, moving, and beautiful energy of the sound waves themselves, which, as you know, stream into your ears and vibrate against your skin, but which also merge with the very energy that *is* your body and mingle with the energy that *is* your tissues, and organs in a way that no surgery, no procedure, and no medicine can.

That's the *physical* dimension of music.

Then there is the matter of music's *emotional* power. Music doesn't just wiggle your eardrums, your skin, and your internal organs; it stirs your mind and soul. It boosts your spirits, makes you happy, lifts you up, and distracts you from pain.

In many ways, music really gets inside you, and, almost as if by magic, it makes things better.

As Sara Hoover, D.M.A., co-director of the Center for Music and Medicine at Johns Hopkins explains: "It's fascinating and powerful to think that music, something that has been floating around in our environment forever, that this natural, omnipresent human activity has demonstrable benefit as treatment."

So, how exactly can music help you? Consider these benefits:

1. Music lowers a patient's stress levels. It calms and soothes. It stimulates positive brain functioning and fosters a general sense of well-being.

2. Music offers remarkable relief from even chronic or intense pain such as that brought about by arthritis. It even decreases one's *perception* of pain.

3. It helps stroke patients recover faster and goes a long way toward helping to restore lost speech.

4. For cancer patients, music reduces the side effects of chemotherapy and radiation therapy. It lowers their levels of anxiety and even helps to reduce nausea.

5. Music improves the outcomes of invasive procedures such as colonoscopies or cardio-angiography. It reduces anxiety and, thus, the need for sedatives. It also helps patients to experience less discomfort.

6. Surgery patients exposed to music—*even while under anesthesia*—will heal faster and need less pain medication during recovery. Yes, even while under anesthesia! Remember, music is energy —energy that your body can absorb, whether you are conscious or not. It needn't flow into your ears and be processed by your conscious mind; it simply has to register with your subconscious mind or vibrate against your skin and, from there, resonate into your entire body.

7. Music can lower blood pressure, heart rate, and respiration rate.

8. In the operating room, music has even been shown to help doctors stay calm, focused, and more able to think clearly and effectively under pressure.

9. Although it would be a stretch to claim that music can directly help to cure serious illnesses such as cancer, it absolutely can help to reduce symptoms, accelerate the healing process, and improve one's quality of life in the process.

To put it more simply: *Music improves medical outcomes virtually across the board.* And it can and will improve yours as well, no matter what medical challenges you face.

Music improves medical outcomes across the board.

So, what can you do to bring the healing power of music into your recovery process?

1. If you are about to undergo surgery, listen to calming, soothing, beautiful music beforehand, especially during pre-op, when you are likely to feel nervous or agitated. Use headphones or earbuds if you are required to do so. Put together a playlist on your phone comprised of soothing and uplifting classical selections (classical music appears to offer the most healing benefit) as well as any other selections

you enjoy, just as long as they are calming and positive. So, yes, I would draw the line at hard rock, heavy metal, and rap—at least until after you're home.

2. Inform your surgeon that you would like music to be playing softly in the operating room during your surgery. If necessary, inform him, or her of music's proven track record of improving the outcome of surgeries.

3. Regardless of whether or not your hospital will allow you to have music in the operating room, insist on having music playing as much as possible during post-op and recovery (again, with headphones or earbuds, if need be).

4. Ask if your hospital offers any music therapy programs—many do. If not, consider enlisting the services of a trained music therapist.

5. Finally, as always, don't forget to *believe* in music's proven power to improve medical outcomes. *Expect* it to work. Fully expect that the music you listen to before, during, and after your surgery—or for the duration of your illness—can

and will go a long way toward easing your pain, improving your condition, and shortening your recovery time.

Firmly believe in the power of music to help you get better.

If you are already in the hospital, it might be difficult to put together a playlist of music. However, you can always search for some good classical music as well as any other calming music you've enjoyed over the years. Try Pandora, XM Radio, Spotify, or YouTube. In fact, on YouTube, you can even search for compilations of classical or New Age music, many of which provide hours of uninterrupted selections already strung together for you.

However, if you are awaiting an upcoming surgery—in other words, if you are not yet being treated—I suggest that you take the time to build a powerful playlist on your phone and bring it with you to the hospital or surgical center. This will go a long way in helping with your healing or recovery process.

Go to iTunes, Spotify, or YouTube Red (a paid service that lets you easily build playlists and download content right into your phone). Then, start searching.

Start with some soothing and beautiful classical music. Pre-screen selections by composers such as J. S. Bach, Frederic Chopin, Claude Debussy, or Eric Satie; all of them are well known for having composed soothing and beautiful music. In any case, nothing heavy, nothing dark.

Next, fill your heart and stir your soul with a sampling of New Age selections by composers such as Enya, Yanni, George Winston, or Mike Oldfield. If you are unfamiliar with New Age music, I suggest that you give it a try. It is similar to classical in its ability to soothe, but it does so with more contemporary harmonies and rhythms, as well as a good dose of free-flowing and mind-stirring improvisation.

Finally, add in selections of your choosing. Again, nothing heavy, dark, or raucous—just songs that make you feel happy and hopeful.

I realize that this requires a bit of time and effort, but considering the power music has in helping you to heal, I'm certain you will find it to be well worth it.

As Bob Marley puts it: "One good thing about music—when it hits you, you feel no pain."

So, let it hit you and hit you good. Let it cheer and becalm you. Let it energize your cells with its magic. Let it get inside you and heal you as nothing else can.

Affirm the Healing Power of Music

Read the following affirmations, silently or aloud, *with conviction and feeling.*

1

I am in awe of the incredible and proven power of music in helping me to heal more quickly and completely.

2

I listen to calming, peaceful, and beautiful music throughout the day during times of illness, and throughout all phases of surgery.

3

I am passionate about music! It stirs my soul. It intoxicates me. It delivers its healing magic to every cell in my body.

4

As I listen, I wholeheartedly feel the music's energy bathing and infusing my body with its healing power.

5

At the same time that music is working its way inside my body, I am crawling inside the music and feeling its melodies, harmonies, and rhythms from the inside out.

6

I am empowered by music. I am made happy by music. I am energized by music. I am made well by music.

7

Music heals my body and heals it well.

8

Music invigorates my soul and strengthens my immune system.

9

I allow myself to fall in love with every aspect of every song I hear. I love and admire the performer. I luxuriate in the beauty of the instruments' sounds. I feel bonded to the melodies, chords, rhythms, harmonies, and lyrics.

10

I fully expect that every song I hear will help reduce my level of pain and anxiety during my hospitalization.

11

I am so grateful for the abundance of healing music in this world. I am grateful for its ability to make me well.

12

As music resonates into my being, I feel its energy mingling with the energy that makes up my body. I feel it enter, cleanse, and heal every cell, every organ, every bone, and every tissue of my being.

13

I take advantage of music's healing power during as many phases of my illness or surgery as possible. As I do, I feel its beauty, power, and healing energy fill me—deeply and completely.

14

I listen to beautiful, calming music before my surgery for its proven ability to reduce anxiety and lessen the need for sedatives.

15

I harness the healing power of music during my surgery, if allowed, and especially during post-op to help me recover faster and with less pain.

16

Given music's centuries-long track-record of success, I have no choice but to fully believe in its power to help me get well again.

17

When I listen to music, I focus intensely on it. I lose myself in it. I try to hear all the different instruments and all the different elements such as rhythm, melody, harmony, and lyrics. I marvel at the brilliance of the composer and the talent of the performers.

18

I "hear" music with my heart. I feel it permeate me. I feel it infuse my spirit with an invigorating and positive energy that makes everything right inside me.

19

I feel each note, each chord, and each beat of every song attach themselves to each cell in my body and fill them with loving energy and healing power.

20

I completely lose myself in the music. I notice all its parts, all the instruments, all its nuances. I focus intensely upon every bar and let it fill me up.

21

I fully expect and believe in the power of music to help accelerate my healing and recovery.

22

I hum or sing along with the music, either silently or audibly, thus deepening my experience and making it part of my physical being.

23

Whenever I am able, I smile appreciatively as the music fills me with its curative magic.

24

I feel a powerful connection with the music I listen to. I am bonded to it. I am one with it.

25

I accept, acknowledge, believe in, and embrace the proven power of music to aid in my healing process.

Healing Actions

Here are three things you can do, starting today, to help you incorporate the incredible power of music into your healing or recovery process:

1. Before. During. After.

If you have an upcoming surgery, listen to soothing, uplifting music before, during, and after the procedure. If you have already had the surgery, listen to music as much as you can to help accelerate your recovery. Do the same if you are suffering from an illness to help your body to heal faster and more completely. And do the same during any procedure or infusion to help you stay calm, reduce nausea, and improve the outcome.

2. Make a playlist

Create a collection of soothing classical and New Age music, along with some of your own favorites to have on hand while you are in the hospital, rehab facility, surgical center, or infusion center. If you are already hospitalized, or you are too weak or tired to make a playlist, just find a station on XM Radio or Pandora, or a channel on YouTube featuring classical or New

Age music. Alternatively, ask a friend or relative to build a playlist for you.

3. Feel it in your soul

To your very core, believe in music's power to help speed your recovery. And while you are listening, feel that music resonate around you, through you, and within you. Feel it deeply— very deeply. Enjoy it passionately. Allow yourself to be moved and mesmerized by it. Feel it in your cells. Feel it in your heart. Feel it with a mind, body, and soul that is filled with joy.

8

Get Weller Sooner with the Power of Affirmations

"I know that I look, feel, and behave several decades younger than my actual age, and much of that is because I believe you are what you think you are. This is called positive affirmation, and it's a really strong tool."

Joan Collins

"It's the repetition of affirmations that leads to belief. And once that belief becomes a deep conviction, things begin to happen."

Claude M. Bristol

So far, in this book, you have been using the power of positive affirmation to help instill each lesson more deeply into your mind-body and to

158

more completely activate each healing strategy. Now, we are going to apply this same affirming power to the process of healing itself.

As I said earlier, the use of affirmations is very widespread among the very successful from all walks of life. It is widespread because affirmations are very powerful and effective in creating a desired outcome.

Oh, but it gets so much better than that! If the use of positive affirmation is so effective in matters *outside* the body, such as the creation of financial or professional success, just imagine what it can do regarding matters *inside* your body. Remember, your body is made by your thoughts *and statements* about it. So, imagine what can happen to the healing and recovery processes going on inside you when they are infused with powerfully positive statements such as those that you will find at the end of this chapter.

If the use of positive affirmation is so effective in matters outside the body, such as financial or professional success, imagine what it can do for matters inside your own body.

We're going to get right down to the nitty-gritty of healing here. You're going to augment and accelerate your healing and recovery by repeating over and over the healing affirmations that I will be sharing with you. And you're going to push them deep into your subconscious and your physical body through *repetition.*

One additional reason for this repetition is because, during times when you may find yourself in pain, nauseous, groggy, or some other state of incapacitation during your illness or recovery, your mind is most likely not going to be at its best. You're going to be tired, uncomfortable, nervous, woozy, and out of sorts. So, you're going to want these affirmations completely memorized (at least some of them) so that even when your mind and body are compromised, you'll have them right there on the tip of your tongue and ready to go.

In short, you want them ingrained deep in your subconscious and, more or less, automatic.

But you have to do things right if you wish to gain maximum benefit from them. Here's how to make affirmations the most powerful, the most healing, and the most effective they can be:

1. *Repeat them.* Read and recite the affirmations many times a day (silently or audibly, as your situation allows). Just

do it and don't let up on it. Affirmations require a lot of repetition, and there is just no way around that. Choose those which resonate with you the most and repeat each one like a mantra.

2. *Believe them.* Strengthen your affirmations further by reciting them with your full *belief* in their power and your *conviction* that they will work.

3. *Feel them.* Whatever positive feelings or emotions you receive from reciting them—*feel* those feelings deeply and intensely. Feel their soothing, healing energy streaming into your body. Feel that energy pushing away pain, disease, weakness, or nausea.

4. *See them.* As you speak them, *visualize* the action or process they describe as happening right inside you. See the affirmations themselves, along with the healing thought-energy they conjure up, as they act upon your pain or illness and remove it from your body. See the diseased cells vanishing. See your incision closing. See your energy and vitality returning.

5. *Record them.* Record the affirmations onto a voice-memo app on your phone and listen to them incessantly. If possible, enlist the services of a loved one or two to record them for you, repeating each one over and over.

6. *Enhance them.* Increase the power and efficacy of affirmations further by having music playing in the background as you recite them. Music aids in learning and what you are trying to do is push these affirmations as deep into your mind as possible. Due to its complexity, as well as its tendency to utilize higher frequencies, classical music works best in helping you to learn.

7. *Write them.* Finally, if it is at all possible, write your favorite affirmations down, over and over, in a notebook. The kinesthetic process of writing will strengthen the learning process even more. But don't worry if you are not up to the task of writing. While beneficial, it is certainly not a necessary step.

Here is the process of affirmation in a nutshell:

1. Repeat them. Daily.

2. Believe in them. Deeply.

3. Feel them. Intensely.

4. Visualize them. Clearly.

5. Record them. Lovingly.

How effective are affirmations? Take two minutes and do a little online research on "affirmations and healing" or some similar search phrase. You will discover an almost infinite number of search results, many from individuals who claim to have healed even terminal cancer using nothing but the incessant repetition of affirmations alone. Again, it is not my place to be speaking on the *validity* or non-validity of such grand claims. But, for goodness' sake, there are *so* many claims of this nature, one can only assume that there must be *something* to them. In any case, the use of affirmations can and will improve your healing or recovery process.

Affirmations can and will improve your healing or recovery process.

Now it's your turn.

Everyone is different. Every medical situation is different. In addition to those that follow this chapter, I urge you to create and recite some of your own affirmations—affirmations which speak directly to you. Try to come up with a half-dozen, but even two or three would be wonderful. Each one should address your specific medical condition or illness. Here are a few examples:

"My heart, although injured by my heart attack, is healing very nicely and growing stronger every day. I am so happy and grateful that my treatments have been very successful in giving me my life back."

"My gallbladder surgery is a success. I am healing very well and ahead of schedule. Thank you."

"This chemotherapy is a lifesaver, and it is thoroughly ridding my body of cancer. I am forever grateful for this medicine."

"I am so happy and grateful that my hip replacement surgery went well and that my recovery is progressing smoothly."

When you create your affirmations, keep these three points in mind:

1. Use the present tense. State your affirmations as if the result you hope to achieve is already happening, or already

has. The use of future tense keeps the desired result exactly there: in the future. Don't say: "I will be well soon." Say: "I *am* well." Don't say: "I will be out of the hospital soon." Say: I *am* out of the hospital, and it feels great!"

2. Use powerful, direct, accurate words. No wishy-washy language. Nothing vague or uncertain.

3. Include a statement of gratitude. As I've said, the Universe gives us more of that for which we are grateful: "I am so happy and grateful now that my tumor is shrinking."

Feel free to edit or rewrite these or any of the affirmations that follow to help get you started. And don't concern yourself in the least with whether or not they are "true" at the present moment. They will *become* true over time; that's all that counts.

It behooves you to start affirming like the dickens as part of your daily healing regimen. And, once again, don't forget to *believe* them. Believe them and believe *in* them—deeply and with absolute certainty.

One more thing:

In recent years, scientists have been learning more and more about the human brain and its amazing properties and capabilities. And one of those properties is referred to as *plasticity.*

Your brain has a whole lot of plasticity. This means that, even as we age, our brains *can* be changed. They can be developed, amended, and even altered by our own volition. And affirmations, it has been learned, can literally alter our brain chemistry.

Just think about that!

Now, that doesn't mean that you can read or utter an affirmation a few times and start moving things around inside your brain (not to mention your body). But with enough persistent repetition, you most certainly can exact changes upon the chemistry of your brain.

And with the affirmations you're about to learn, this altered brain chemistry can and will work wonders upon your body with the help of your powerful mind-body connection   one that has been turbocharged with powerful words and statements of strength and healing.

Let's close this chapter with something special. What follows is a long-form affirmation for you to recite at least twice a day. My wish for you is that it will heal you in ways that nothing else can.

And don't forget to read it often, read it aloud (if only at a whisper), read it with feeling, read it with conviction, and read it with an expectation of success!

The healing energy of the Universe manifests as thoughts of strength, comfort, and wellness in my mind. These thoughts then manifest as powerful healing energies which, in turn, bring about strength, comfort, and wellness throughout my body.

Through my thoughts of strength, I see myself as strong, I feel strong, and my body grows strong.

Through my thoughts of comfort, I see myself without pain or discomfort, I feel fabulous, and my body grows ever more at peace.

Through my thoughts of transcendence, I see myself moving beyond this illness or surgery, I feel myself moving beyond this illness or surgery, and my body returns to a state of wellness and vitality.

I see, therefore I feel, pain leaving my body.

I see, therefore I feel, disease leaving my body.

I see, therefore I feel, strength returning to my body.

I see, therefore I feel, good health, vitality, and a bolstered spirit returning to my body.

My bones are well.

My organs are well.

My tissues are well.

My cells are well.

My mind is well.

My soul is well.

My being is well.

My body is now completely healed, and I am forever grateful for my skilled doctors, my caring nurses, my successful surgery, my effective medications, my powerful mind, my Creator, the support of my loved ones, and the ever-present healing energy that permeates the Universe for all they have done for me. Thank you!

Affirm Healing in Your Body

Read the following affirmations, silently or aloud, *with conviction and feeling.*

1

When I have an illness, even a serious illness, I use the incredible, well-known power of affirmations to help bring about my rapid recovery.

2

I am grateful now that my body is healthy, strong, perfect, and healed.

3

My powerful and skilled immune system is hard at work at right now, killing my disease, healing my incision, rebuilding my strength, and making me well.

4

I am grateful now that my illness is receding, my incision is closing, my appetite is returning, my strength is returning, my pain is diminishing, my prognosis is brightening, and my condition is improving every day.

5

Every cell in my body is, once again, vibrating with healthful and vital energy.

6

In my mind's eye, I see pure, soothing, healing energy streaming into my body, ridding it of pain.

7

I feel powerful, healing energy coursing throughout my body, killing disease, making me strong.

8

Every muscle, every organ, every cell in my body is filled with wellness and vitality.

9

I see the diseased cells in my body being destroyed by the millions thanks to my doctors, my medicines, my immune system, and the benevolent, healing energy that permeates the Universe.

10

I have the intention, the power, and the tenacity to beat and heal quickly from any illness.

11

My mind, my body, and my will are infinitely more powerful than the collection of viral or bacterial germs taking up residence inside me at this moment.

12

Throughout every minute of the day, I feel my body growing stronger, more healed, more cleansed, more fit, more robust, more energized, more vital, and more perfect.

13

I feel great! I feel wonderful! I feel strong! I feel better than ever!

14

I am grateful for my immune system. It is powerful, intelligent, capable, and effective at ridding my body of illness.

15

Powerful healing energy is coming to me from all corners of the Universe, infusing my body with everything it needs to be well again.

16

I call upon and receive energy from the Universe. I see and feel it merge with the energy of my body and remove all of its negative energies, be they sadness, anger, fear, weakness, injury, or disease.

17

I am stronger than this illness. I am larger than this illness. I am more powerful than this illness. I am more tenacious than this or any illness.

18

I am completely healed. I am well once again. Every part of my body is tingling with wellness. I am filled with gratitude for my return to good health.

19

I expect my treatments to work. I expect my medications to work. I expect my body's healing power to do its job.

20

Every day, I feel the healing energies of strength, loving connection, and positive expectation permeate my body with all that it needs to be well again.

21

Every day I feel gratitude for my doctors, nurses, treatments, and medicines. The Universe gives us more of that which we are grateful for, and I am eternally grateful for all that has been done to bring healing and recovery to me.

22

I use these and other positive affirmations to aid in my healing with the full conviction that they will work, they will work well, and they will work wonders.

23

I am open to receive the many powerful energies that surround, enfold, and infuse my being with all that I need to be well again.

24

My illness is made of energy. My mind, body, and spirit are made of energy as well—and these are infinitely more powerful than the energy that comprises any illness that may enter my system.

25

I accept, acknowledge, believe in, and embrace the proven power of positive affirmation to aid in my healing process.

Finally, here is the long-form affirmation once again:

The healing energy of the Universe manifests as thoughts of strength, comfort, and wellness in my mind. These thoughts then manifest as powerful healing energies which, in turn, bring about strength, comfort, and wellness throughout my body.

Through my thoughts of strength, I see myself as strong, I feel strong, and my body grows strong.

Through my thoughts of comfort, I see myself without pain or discomfort, I feel fabulous, and my body grows ever more at peace.

Through my thoughts of transcendence, I see myself moving beyond this illness or surgery, I feel myself moving beyond this illness or surgery, and my body returns to a state of wellness and vitality.

I see, therefore I feel, pain leaving my body.

I see, therefore I feel, disease leaving my body.

I see, therefore I feel, strength returning to my body.

I see, therefore I feel, good health, vitality, and a bolstered spirit returning to my body.

My bones are well.

My organs are well.

My tissues are well.

My cells are well.

My mind is well.

My soul is well.

My being is well.

My body is now completely healed, and I am forever grateful for my skilled doctors, my caring nurses, my successful surgery, my effective medications, my powerful mind, my Creator, the support of my loved ones, and the ever-present healing energy that permeates the Universe for all they have done for me. Thank you.

Healing Actions

Here are three things you can do, starting today, to help you better capitalize on the incredible healing power of positive affirmation:

1. Read your affirmations

Read them over and over, aloud, or to yourself. State them with your hand over your heart and in a firm voice filled with conviction. Study the affirmations from this chapter and feel their energy stream inside you. As you do, remind yourself of the enormous track record of success that affirmations have had among countless thousands of people. Believe every one with all your heart. Feel their power throughout your body. Expect them to work. Be confident that they will work. Maintain an unwavering conviction that they will work.

2. Record your affirmations

Record the affirmations from this chapter (and all other chapters as well) onto a voice memo app on your phone. If possible, or if you're not up to it, ask a friend or loved one to record them for you. Pop some headphones on and listen to them often throughout the day. Even while you're asleep. Set the recording to play over and over. Your subconscious mind will receive them and work with them, even when your conscious mind is turned off.

3. Create your own affirmations

Write and memorize at least six affirmations of your own that are specific to your situation. Use powerful, positive, present-tense language. They needn't be perfect or grammatically correct. They simply need to affirm your healing and recovery in any way that seems right to you. Write them on an index card to keep nearby, or type them into a note-taking app on your phone.

9

Get Weller Sooner with the Power of Good Nutrition

"Let food be thy medicine and medicine be thy food."

Hippocrates

"Today, more than 95% of all chronic disease is caused by food choice, toxic food ingredients, nutritional deficiencies, and lack of physical exercise."

Mike Adams: Publisher, Natural News

Pardon me for stating the obvious, but...

You are what you eat. You are entirely *what you eat.*

Yes, you've undoubtedly heard this before, but let's delve deeper into this assertion.

Since virtually every cell in your body is replaced within seven years (and most of them are replaced much sooner than that), it is not at all a stretch to say that virtually every cell in your body is made from something you've eaten during the last seven years' time.

You are made entirely of the food you've eaten within the past seven years.

You are made entirely of the food you've eaten within the past seven years.

Excuse the redundancy, but I hope that the above statement has made an impression upon you because, when it comes to matters of health and well-being—*all* matters of health and well-being, in fact—food is at the top of the list. And from this, it becomes more than obvious that, when it comes to matters of *your* healing and recovery, food should absolutely be at the top of your list.

It comes down to two duties on your part:

1. Eat the very best food you can.

I understand that this is not always possible, if, say, you're on a liquid diet, or perhaps some highly limited, highly regimented diet prescribed by your doctors. But, otherwise, do the best you can—and this goes for when you're in the hospital as well as after you're home recuperating.

How? First, when given choices for your meals, *opt for the good choice*. Good choices include:

- Avoiding the more over-processed, junky, non-nutritious offerings. Seriously, when it comes to matters of health and healing, hot dogs, cookies, and chips are, for all intents and purposes, garbage—and I promise you that they will do your healing no good whatsoever. Avoid this stuff—not "as if" your life depends on it—but *because* your life depends on it.

- Getting your hands on anything organic as much as possible. If pesticides don't do pests much good, they won't do you much good, either. Poison and healing—not a winning combination.

- Avoiding chemicals: preservatives, colors, artificial ingredients, and other additives. Much of what you are given won't come with a list of ingredients, of course. But some of it will be packaged, and you would do well to avoid "foods" with ingredients you can't pronounce, let alone describe. Like fitness guru, Jack Lalanne, once said: "If man made it, don't eat it!"

- Avoiding, to the greatest extent possible, foods grown with GMOs (genetically modified organisms). With packaged food like chips, granola bars, and so on, if it doesn't say "Made without GMO's" clearly on the package, chances are it has them. With so many non-GMO options available nowadays, there is absolutely no reason to take your chances with anything else.

- Focusing on lean proteins and plant-based foods as much as possible.

- To the greatest extent possible, avoiding what success expert, Brian Tracy, refers to as "the three white poisons": sugar, salt, and white flour. None of these will do your physiology a bit of good, to say the least, especially when you're trying to get better.

- Focusing on *whole foods*, that is, foods that are unprocessed or minimally processed. Choosing an orange over orange juice, for example. Opting for a baked potato over chips or fries. Avoiding anything that you suspect was probably conjured up in a lab, not a kitchen.

First bottom line: Don't be compromising your body with anything less than the best food you can obtain. Ask if your hospital has a licensed nutritionist on staff who can steer you in the right direction with your food choices and eating protocols. If not, you will need to make good food choices yourself. Remember, you are made entirely out of what you eat and drink, so please "make" yourself from the best ingredients you can get.

Eat the very best food you can, to the greatest extent you can.

Now, here come the arguments:

"I've just been through (or am about to go through) a terrible ordeal! I'm *entitled* to a little comfort (read "junk") food!"

Well, that all depends. If you're saying that a yummy snack from time to time is within your "rights" as a healing patient, I'm not going to argue with you. But I caution you to reconsider the notion of using junk food as some sort of reward. And in any case, it is most certainly not in the best interests of your healing process.

Furthermore, enjoying an *occasional* treat is an altogether different matter than choosing your regular meals and snacks comprised of food whose sole purpose is the momentary entertainment of your tongue, rather than nourishing, healing, and creating your irre-placeable, non-returnable body.

Next argument: "I'm in the hospital! I can't always get healthful food in the first place."

Again, that all depends. First, have you asked? Have you inquired as to whether they might have some fruit available instead of that bag of Sun Chips? It never hurts to ask.

Second, while your hospital might not nec-essarily have the best choices available, you can nonetheless make *better* choices from among those they do offer.

Third, if you have any visitors at all, let them know that your healing can be positively influenced with the help of healthful food, and so would they mind bringing you some? How about fresh blueberries (very high in healing antioxidants) or other fruit? How about some raw carrots or celery? Perhaps some healthful juices or Greek yogurt? Or how about a box of really good, whole-grain cereal? The hospital can certainly get you some milk to pour on.

Second bottom line: Put as much food into your body as you possibly can that is beneficial, not detrimental, to your health, particularly while your body's well-being is compromised. You're trying to make things better for yourself, not worse.

And finally, if you're trying to regain your strength, you need to eat, period. If you just can't seem to keep things down, keep trying. Hopefully, you can find even one or two things that arc bland enough to not make you sick. Do everything you possibly can to get yourself to eat, to eat enough, and to eat well.

2. Believe in your food.

I'm reminding you once again that your beliefs and especially your expectations go a long way toward enhancing the power of every healing strategy in this book.

Do you want your mind to better affect the goings-on inside your body, as I explained in Chapter 1? Then *believe* in that power. Expect your body to respond in accordance with your thinking. Know with all your heart that your healing will be accelerated and improved by directing your body to heal using the power of your mind—in other words, by your *expecting* to heal.

Do you want your positive thinking to do the same, as explained in Chapter 2? Then *believe* in that power as well. Expect your positive thinking to have a positive effect on your healing and recovery.

Likewise, you need to believe in the power of harnessing your inner strength, as we discussed in Chapter 4, and to expect it to help you to get well.

Ditto for behaving as the perfect patient (Chapter 5): *Believe* in this practice, too. Expect it to help you.

Ditto for calling upon the power of laughter and music (Chapters 6 and 7) to help make you well. *Expect* it to do just that.

Believe in and expect the best from all the techniques you've learned thus far, as well as those still to come. This will significantly strengthen their ability to help you get better.

And, yes, the same goes for the food you eat. If you're going to nourish your body with food and strengthen your body with food and build new cells with food, then give your food a little help by believing in its power to help you. Expect the best from the food you eat, and you will get the best right back—assuming, of course, that you're eating good food.

Remember Hippocrates' wise words at the start of this chapter: *"Let food be thy medicine and medicine be thy food."*

Firmly believe in the power of your food to help make you well.

One final and very important point:

Always remember that my intention for you regarding every strategy in this book is that they will be used *in conjunction with* whatever standard medical care you are receiving. Even though many individuals claim to have been cured or healed using one or more of these strategies alone and without medical inter-vention, and regardless of the fact that many of these people can prove it, I caution you to try no such thing. You need to give your body every advantage it can get, and these include the professional care of your doctors as well as any medications prescribed to you.

The same goes for the food you eat during your recovery and healing process. While it may be true (and while I may agree) that many individuals have cured themselves of everything from depression to asthma to liver disease to terminal cancer using nutrition-based protocols planned out by competent, trained profession-als, please do no such thing. Give your body *every* advantage you can, excluding nothing—particularly treatments and medications prescribed by your doctor—*even if* you are convinced that the strategies in this book alone will do the trick.

The purpose of this book is to *supplement* standard medical care with proven strategies that will augment or enhance this care. This will result in an improvement in your outcome, whether by incurring less pain, scoring a shorter hospital stay or recovery period, enduring a less harrowing illness, or enjoying more certain and complete healing.

Using food to aid in your healing and recovery process in tandem with everything your medical team can give and everything this book can provide will give you virtually every advantage and every edge you could possibly have.

So, please, at least for the duration of your hospitalization, eat solely for improved recovery and nothing more.

Instead of deriving "comfort" from your food, how about deriving nutrition from your food and comfort from the process of getting weller sooner?

Affirm the Healing Power of Good Nutrition

Read the following affirmations, silently or aloud, *with conviction and feeling.*

1

I am what I eat. I am literally and entirely what I eat.

2

What I eat is what I am. My food isn't just inside me—it *is* me.

3

I want to heal quickly, and I understand that good food plays a key role in that process.

4

Bad food, rich food, junk food, and chemical-laden food of any kind is not in my best interest, especially when I am weak or ill.

5

I'm well aware that the quality of the food that goes inside me ultimately becomes the quality of me.

6

The food I eat creates my body; I choose what I eat with the utmost care.

7

I eat to create my body and to nourish my body, not for the sole purpose of momentarily amusing my tongue.

8

Especially while in the hospital, I make smart, well-researched food choices.

9

I am important, and I am what I eat. Thus, what I eat is profoundly important.

10

I strongly believe that the good food I eat is directly and powerfully connected to my rapid and successful recovery.

11

While recovering from illness or surgery, I feed my body the very best food I can to help speed my healing.

12

One of the best ways I can accelerate my body's ability to heal is by avoiding chemical-laden food as much as possible. Chemical food-additives are not necessary, they are toxic, and they have no business inside me.

13

I'm aware that good food is simply another form of medicine.

14

I fully expect the good food I eat to help make me well. I firmly believe in the healing power of good nutrition.

15

As I eat, I visualize my body growing stronger and healthier from my food.

16

As I eat, I visualize the food infusing my body with vitality, strength, and wellness.

17

As I eat, I visualize the cells of my body growing ever more healed and ever more empowered.

18

My body is far too precious for me to nourish it with anything but the best food I can.

19

I am continually aware that every cell in my body is made from something I've eaten during the past few years—and I choose my food accordingly.

20

I eat wisely and responsibly. I eat with my body's best interest in mind.

21

With each bite I swallow, I feel my body being made stronger and healthier by it.

22

I eat with the conviction that my food is helping me to heal faster and to stay healthy.

23

I am what I eat. I am entirely what I eat. I am forever what I eat.

24

I don't mess around with food. In its own way, my food is medicine, and I choose it with the same care my doctor takes in prescribing medicine to me.

25

I accept, acknowledge, believe in, and embrace the proven power of good nutrition to aid in my healing process.

Healing Actions

Here are three things you can do, starting today, to help you derive maximum healing benefit from the food you eat:

1. Understand the importance of nutrition

Cone to fully understand that every cell in your body is replaced within seven years; every cell, therefore, is something you've eaten within the last seven years. If you want the forty to fifty billion new cells that you replace every day to be made healthy, strong, and vital, make sure they are made from the very best food you can.

2. Eat with healing in mind

To the greatest extent possible: Avoid foods containing artificial or chemical *anything*— preservatives, colors, flavor "enhancers," and GMOs. Focus on plants (fruits, veggies, berries, seeds), lean sources of protein (fish, poultry), and minimally-processed whole foods. Ask your doctors, nurses, and (if available) a nutritionist for suggestions on how to get the most healing benefit from food.

3. Believe in your food

Know that with each bite of good food you eat, you are doing your body good. Know that eating well will build you well and heal you well. Eat with the conviction and full-on expectation that the healthful food you eat is, in its own way, medicine.

10

Get Weller Sooner with the Power of Medicine

"Give someone who has faith in you a placebo and call it a hair growing pill, anti-nausea pill or whatever, and you will be amazed at how many respond to your therapy."
Bernie Siegel

"Medications almost always do it better if they're used in conjunction with other supports."
Mehmet Oz

When you think about it, there are essentially four kinds of medicines:

1. Those that work.

2. Those that don't *really* work, but, ultimately, they work anyway because we *expect* them to.

3. Those that don't work.

4. Those that really *do* work, but, ultimately, they don't work because we *don't expect* them to.

In other words, *believing* that a medicine will work—*expecting it to work*—goes a long way toward helping it to work. On the other hand, *not* believing that a medicine will work—*expecting it not to work*—goes a long way toward rendering it ineffective.

And you know what that means...

Right, it's that same mind-body connection phenomenon again:

Believing that a medicine (real or fake) can help you and even cure you, and expecting it to do so, sends powerfully positive messages to your body, and, most important, to your body's own natural self-healing mechanisms, which, in turn, help to bring about the very healing processes you need most.

Expecting a medicine to work sends powerfully positive messages to your body's own natural self-healing mechanisms.

Well, then, is it the *medicine itself* that does the healing? Or, does your *belief* in the medicine's ability serve to activate your body's own ability to heal itself?

To varying degrees, both are correct. Sometimes medicines really do work exactly as promised, and they do so on a purely physiological, cellular, or chemical level. But sometimes it is nothing but the belief in the medicine that does the job.

And your belief in the medicine, along with your body's own natural ability to heal, will significantly help the situation either way.

As you may have guessed, this brings us to the subject of the *placebo effect*.

As I mentioned in the first chapter, the placebo effect has been proven, time and again, to work. Give a patient a sugar pill and tell them it is a powerful pain medicine, and very often, the pain will subside. The placebo effect is a very real biological response, and research confirms this.

Here is how Bruce H. Lipton, Ph.D. puts it:

"If the brain expects that a treatment will work, it sends healing chemicals into the bloodstream, which facilitates that. That's why the placebo effect is so powerful for every type of healing. And the opposite is equally true and equally powerful: When the brain expects that a therapy will not work, it doesn't. It's called the *nocebo* effect."

When it comes to medicine, real or fake, your expectations make all the difference.

> **When it comes to medicine, your expectations make all the difference.**

But here is a big "but":

Bear in mind that placebos don't always work. Believing that a sugar pill will cure one's cancer or some other serious illness has never been proven to work (which is not to say that it has never worked; it just hasn't been proven scientifically). In any case, you are strongly advised to put your faith in real medicine, not a placebo. And when you do, know full-well that the medicine's power to help you will be maximized and even enhanced by *your faith in its ability to do so*.

To put it another way: No matter what medicine you are given or is prescribed to you, take that medicine with the full faith and conviction that it will work. One way or another, through the medicine's chemical capabilities, your body's natural ability to heal, or a combination of the two, your faith, conviction, and positive expectation will turbocharge that medicine's inherent capabilities.

Take your medicine with the full faith and conviction that it will work.

Look at it this way: If your belief in a placebo can often bring about an improvement in your medical condition, just imagine what your firm belief in a _real_ medicine can do!

Here is how to get the maximum benefit from the medicines you are given:

1. _Get the best._ Whether you are advised to take a prescription medication, an over-the-counter product, or a homeopathic preparation, get the one with the best track-record of safety and efficacy, and the one from the most reputable manufacturer. Ask your doctor, talk to a pharmacist, and do your own research. Don't skimp on your medicines. This is not the time to be penny-pinching.

2. *Take it exactly as you are told to take it*: How much. At what time(s) of day. Before a meal or after a meal. Don't skimp and don't skip. These seemingly insignificant infractions can go a long way toward weakening or even destroying the medicine's potential ability to help you. Worse, they can hurt you, worsen your condition, and even kill you. Don't play around with medicine in any way whatsoever.

3. *Trust in your doctor.* This is more important than you may think. In fact, a primary criterion for even a placebo's ability to fix us up lies in our sincere trust in our doctor's recommendations. Trusting in one's doctor is, of course, simply another facet in the realm of belief and expectation and it is purely a matter of choice—a simple decision on your part—and nothing more. So, make the smart choice and put your full confidence and trust in your doctor.

4. *Every time you take the medicine, affirm its power and efficacy.* Tell yourself: "This is good medicine and it will help me. I have complete faith in its power to do so."

5. *After you take it, continue to believe in the medicine's power.* Know that it will work. Trust in it. Expect it to work. See it working. Visualize that medicine ridding your body of pain, nausea, illness, disease, or whatever other undesirable condition has taken up residence inside you. See the pill or the liquid surrounding the unwelcome intruder and destroying it. See your organs healing. See your muscles functioning normally once again and without pain. See the various affected parts of your body returning to their normal robust state. Just imagine these as best you can. It doesn't matter in the least whether or not your mental images are "accurate" or "correct." Just visualize all the above in whatever way makes the most sense and seems the most effective, then let your body take it from there.

6. *Also, using your imagination, feel yourself healing and your condition improving as a result of having taken the medicine.* Remember how connected your body is to your thinking (imagination). Imagine how it will feel to be well again. Then, through this connection,

you will soon experience it for real in the outer dimension.

So, be a good patient and take your medicine. Just don't forget to help the medicine along by taking it exactly as prescribed and by maintaining a firm belief in its efficacy. You do your part, and the medicine will take it from there.

Affirm the Healing Power of Medicine

Read the following affirmations, silently or aloud, *with conviction and feeling*.

1

I take all my medications precisely as I am instructed by my doctor.

2

I take all medications I am given with the firm conviction that they will work to the greatest extent possible.

3

I choose to firmly and fully believe in the power of the medicines I am given.

4

I expect the best from all my medications.

5

I am fully aware that the medicines I take will work more or less in accord with my expectations.

6

My body responds well to all the medicines I receive, in part because that is what I expect it to do.

7

My medications are powerful; my positive expectations make them even more powerful.

8

I operate from the premise that every drug I am given is a wonder drug.

9

I expect to feel a whole lot better very soon; thanks to the medicines I am taking.

10

I use the power of my imagination to visualize every pill and potion I take going to work immediately, powerfully, and effectively.

11

In my mind's eye, I see my medicine eradicating any pain I may have.

12

In my mind's eye, I see my medicine destroying the disease that has invaded my body.

13

In my mind's eye, I see my medication flooding my body with healing, strength, and wellness.

14

I fully trust in my doctor's decision to prescribe this medication to me.

15

I am grateful for all the medicines I take.

16

This medicine permeates my body with healing. My expectations for healing do the same. Together, they are unbeatable.

17

To my core, I trust in the power of the medicine I am now taking.

18

I am convinced that this medication will do its job and do it well.

19

I know, without a trace of doubt, that this prescription will help me to get well.

20

I can feel this medication surging through my bloodstream, then throughout my entire body, carrying with it the power to greatly improve my medical condition.

21

My condition is improving by the day, thanks to the powerful medicines I am taking.

22

The medicine I am now taking is moving directly to the source of my pain or illness, and it will eliminate it.

23

I have no doubt whatsoever that my medicines will work exactly as promised.

24

I trust my doctor. I trust in my medicine. I trust in my mind to augment the power of my medicine through positive expectation and visualization.

25

I accept, acknowledge, believe in, and embrace the proven power of all medicines I am given to aid in my healing process.

Healing Actions

Here are three things you can do, starting today, to help you get the most from the medications you are given.

1. Take your medicine responsibly
Take it exactly as directed and as often as directed.

2. Take your medicine trustingly
Flood your mind with nothing but positive expectations that it will work as well as expected and even better than expected.

3. Take your medicine mindfully
Every time you take your medication, visualize it going to work. See it doing its job: eliminating pain, healing your illness, eradicating your disease, alleviating symptoms, and making you well. Visualize with bright, bold, detailed im-ages—and visualize often. Your powerful mind-body connection will do the rest.

11

Get Weller Sooner with the Power of Prayer

"Prayer is man's greatest power!"
W. Clement Stone

"Faith and prayer are the vitamins of the soul; man cannot live in health without them."
Mahalia Jackson

Even amongst the most cynical and least spiritual individuals, the extraordinary and well-documented power of prayer in healing from illness or recovery after surgery can no longer be denied. Study after study—more than 1200 to date—have given researchers and doctors an irrefutable array of clinical data to support the statement that prayer really and truly does heal.

These studies consistently indicate that prayer offers significant improvement in a host of medical situations including heart disease, Parkinson's disease, and even cancer, as well as improved and accelerated healing after surgery of any kind.

Now consider these statistics, reported by Jeanie Lerche Davis, from WebMD:

- Hospitalized people who never attended church have an average stay of three times longer than people who attend regularly.

- In Israel, elderly people who never or rarely attend church have a forty percent higher death rate from cardiovascular disease and cancer.

- Elderly people who never or rarely attend church have a stroke rate double that of people who attend regularly.

And according to Harold G. Koenig, M.D., of Duke University, as reported in Newsmax Health:

"Studies have shown that prayer can prevent people from getting sick—and when they do get sick, prayer can help them get better faster."

"Studies have shown that prayer can prevent people from getting sick—and when they do get sick, prayer can help them get better faster." - Harold G. Koenig, M.D.

Now, of course, there are numerous theories—some speculative and some supported by science—as to how and why prayer works. Here are two of the most important ones:

First, there is the act of praying itself. When we pray to a Higher Power for an end to our suffering, or at least aid in our healing, we are, in fact, meditating. Prayer is a form of meditation, one with a spiritual twist. The process of this meditation releases positive, healing energy into our body, along with healing chemicals that strengthen the immune response.

Next, there is the matter of a Higher Power. Remember in Chapter 1, when I spoke of "quantum physics"? Here you learned that one of the chief tenets of this branch of science is that matter is made of energy and energy, in turn, is made of intelligence.

Well, another principal component of quantum science is that everything—and I mean every single blessed thing in the Universe—is *connected*. And that "everything" includes your body. When a patient prays or is prayed for by others, these prayers radiate outward in the form of *energy* and attract to it other like energies. This happens quite easily and naturally since, as I said, all things—all energies—are already connected.

> ***When a patient prays or is prayed for by others, these prayers radiate outward in the form of energy and attract other like energies.***

And one of those energies is God, or Allah, or Yahweh, or Universal Intelligence, or whatever name you choose to call your Creator. So, first of all, prayers connect you to the Divine.

Of course, there can be no scientifically attained "proof" that God or any Higher Power brought about the healing. But when you boil the concept of "God" down to its core, you have, once again, *energy*. And the interconnectedness of energies throughout the cosmos *has* been proven.

In addition to that, and in addition to those 1200 studies on prayer in healing, you have a mountain of anecdotal "evidence" from throughout the world to consider. If there are perhaps millions of cases in which it would appear that prayer has "worked" to help people heal faster and better, then certainly these claims can't all be erroneous, now can they? And that's good enough for me—and for millions of others as well—proven on paper or not.

Regardless of the *reason* behind the ability of prayer to increase or even bring about healing, you would do well to pray for your own healing—every day. When something works, you don't need a reason.

But don't stop there because praying for one's own healing isn't even the biggest or best part. Here's where the whole idea of *healing prayer* gets really good:

Group prayer.

Many of the studies involving prayer in healing were centered around patients who were, unbeknown to them, prayed for by a circle of others. Sometimes these others were friends and family members; sometimes, they were strangers from other parts of the world. When the collective energy of others is harnessed on your behalf, you can most certainly expect to get weller sooner.

When the collective energy of others is harnessed on your behalf, you can most certainly expect to get weller sooner.

Here's how you can put together a very powerful prayer circle to aid in your healing and recovery process (note: if you are not up to this task, please ask someone close to you to take it on).

1. *Team up.* Call together as large a group of people as possible—people who know and care about you. These include friends and family members, of course, but take it further than that. Ask coworkers, neighbors, friends of friends, your barber or hairdresser, and the waitress at your favorite cafe. Ask all of them to pray for you. Then, go all the way by asking all of them to ask others from their circles as well. Think *viral* here.

2. *Spread the word.* Use any form of social media you can to drum up support for your prayer circle. When my sister-in-law was diagnosed with stage-four ovarian cancer, her daughters immediately set up a Facebook page titled:

Positive Energy for Christina. It was initially a means by which to spread the word about her newly forming prayer circle. Now, it functions primarily as a place for members to offer supportive words, quotes, ideas, pictures, and resources to help in her fight. And, despite the advanced stage of her cancer when it was first diagnosed, she continues to function and flourish to this day.

3. *Set a prayer schedule.* Once you have a group assembled, pick a morning and evening time, say, 7:00 a.m. and 9:00 p.m., at which times everyone will offer his or her prayers. Members can, of course, pray at their own chosen times instead, but that group energy coming together at the same moment in time will be a force to reckon with. This schedule will begin immediately and continue until you are well. If you are to undergo surgery or some other major procedure, schedule an extra "prayer session" to take place during that particular time as well. Advise the members of your circle to set daily alarms on their phones, reminding them when it's time to pray.

4. *Pick your prayers.* Offer a few healing prayers for everyone to choose from (or they can use their own). You can find a multitude of both religious and secular prayers for healing on the Internet to suit any faith. Choose those you like best and email them to everyone. Invite them to search for their own if they prefer. I have included several healing prayers at the end of this chapter as well.

5. *See and feel the prayers working.* At the scheduled prayer time, or whenever you are able, direct your attention outward, then inward. Feel all these energies coming to you from the outside, from everyone in your circle. Then, picture these loving, healing energies enfolding you and flowing inside your body. Feel them heal you, strengthen you, and cleanse you. Feel every part of your body receiving these prayers and responding with a warm, pulsating glow of strength and wellness.

6. *Expect the prayers to work!* Fully and completely. Know in your heart and soul that prayer has aided countless individuals in their healing, and it will help you, too!

7. *Be thankful for the prayers you have just received.* I remind you again that the Universe gives you more of that which you are grateful for. Feel gratitude for the efforts of everyone who prays on your behalf. Feel healed not only by the prayers themselves but by the love-energy that brought these prayers to you.

Again, there are myriad prayers of healing to be found on the Internet. A five-minute Google search will most certainly yield more than enough to aid in your recovery and medical well-being.

Meanwhile, here are a few to get started with.

This first prayer is of the Christian faith and is for your personal use:

Loving God, I pray to You for strength, comfort, and healing throughout my recovery process. I pray that You will provide assistance to my doctors, in whatever form may be needed, as they work to heal my body. May Your loving, merciful power fill every cell of my body and every layer of my soul with pure, blessed, healing energy. I place my full, grateful, and loving trust in Your power as well as that of our Savior, Jesus Christ. Amen.

Here is one for you to offer to the members of your prayer circle. It is the same prayer as the first, but reworded for the use of others praying on your behalf:

Loving God, I pray to You for strength, comfort, and healing of (your name) throughout his/her recovery process. I pray that You will provide assistance to his/her doctors, in whatever form may be needed, as they work to heal his/her body. May Your loving, merciful power fill every cell of (your name)'s body and every layer of his/her soul with pure, blessed, healing energy. I place my full, grateful, and loving trust in Your power as well as that of our Savior, Jesus Christ. Amen.

The final prayers are spiritual in nature; they are not based upon a specific religious faith. The first is for your use; the last two are for the use of your prayer circle:

With my loving spirit and grateful heart, I call upon the healing power of the Universe to infuse every cell of my being with powerful, benevolent healing energy. I ask that my medical team be empowered with all that they need to ensure my rapid and full recovery. I trust in the wisdom of the Universal mind to provide me with all the strength, self-assuredness, courage, and tenacity I may need throughout my healing process, and I am forever grateful for all the wellness I am to receive. Thank you with all my heart.

With my loving spirit and grateful heart, I call upon the healing power of the Universe to infuse every cell of (your name)'s being with powerful, benevolent healing energy. I ask that his/her medical team be empowered with all that they need to ensure his/her rapid and full recovery. I trust in the wisdom of the Universal mind to provide (your name) with all the strength, self-assuredness, courage, and tenacity s/he may need throughout his/her healing process, and I am forever grateful for all the wellness s/he is to receive. Thank you with all my heart.

The positive, loving, powerful, healing energy in my soul is now streaming into the body and soul of (your name). This energy can and will ease his/her pain and suffering and remove sickness and disease from his/her body. I call upon all the loving and healing energy that fills the Universe to join with mine and provide a potent measure of comfort and healing for him/her. I trust in this energy to

*heal. I put all my sincere faith in this energy. I
send forth this energy upon a wave of deep,
unconditional love for (your name).*

As I type these words, I too am calling upon all
the Powers that Be to fill you with all the warm,
pure, white light of healing energy you may need
for a rapid and total recovery from your illness
or surgery. I am sending a wave of loving prayer
and good wishes on your behalf, and I trust that
this wave will join with the energy of our
Creator, along with the energies of your loved
ones, and stream directly to your aid.

Affirm the Power of Prayer in Your Healing Process

Read the following affirmations, silently or aloud, *with conviction and feeling*.

1

I understand that the power of prayer in speeding my recovery from either surgery or illness is very well-documented. I fully and firmly believe and trust in this power.

2

I enlist family and friends to form a prayer circle on my behalf. I ask them to pray for me to improve the outcome of my recovery and healing.

3

Given the enormous volume of research proving the power of prayer, I have no choice but to fully trust in its efficacy—this results in even greater healing for me.

4

I feel deep, heartfelt, unconditional love for all who pray on my behalf.

5

I expect miracles. I understand that to expect miracles is to help bring them about.

6

When I know that loved ones are praying for me, I visualize and feel the power of their collective prayer coursing through my body, filling it with love, giving it strength, and helping me to heal faster and more completely.

7

I see and feel the prayers of my loved ones infusing my being with powerful, healing energy.

8

I feel and visualize the prayers of my loved ones streaming into my body and eliminating disease, pain, and weakness.

9

I feel the healing energy set forth by my loved ones, in the form of prayer, as it enters my body and gives me the strength to heal, the motivation to fight my illness, and the faith to persevere.

10

When I know that others are praying for me, I fill my mind, body, and soul with gratitude for the powerful, loving, healing energy being sent my way.

11

I visualize the powerful, positive, and healing spirit of prayer as a pure, white light that surrounds my being with a shield of healing energy.

12

Each time I inhale, I visualize the healing energy of prayer, filling me with renewed good health and vitality.

13

Each time I exhale, I visualize the healing energy of prayer carrying toxins, disease, pain, and negative energy away from my ever-strengthening body.

14

I understand the proven benefits of prayer— and my body, created by my thoughts, grows ever stronger, ever more vital, and ever healthier.

15

I send my healing prayers outward upon a wave of love. I receive the prayers of my friends and family in the very same way.

16

I am overwhelmed by joy and gratitude as I receive the healing prayers of my loved ones.

17

Whether in a church, in nature, or my own private practice, spirituality is an important part of my life.

18

My God (or Creator, or Universal Power) is with me at all times throughout my illness (or surgery, or recovery), lending comfort, strength, hope, and resilience.

19

I connect deeply with a higher power. I am protected by my higher power. I am healed by my higher power.

20

My higher power isn't just near me; it envelops me and is present within me.

21

I repeat the words of my favorite healing prayer, silently or audibly, many times throughout my day as a sustaining and life-giving mantra.

22

I fully expect the proven power of prayer to aid greatly in my healing process.

23

I trust in the power of prayer. I have full faith in the power of prayer. I have a firm, unwavering conviction that prayer is a powerful healing force.

24

I know deep in my soul that the prayers of my loved ones will help me to see this through.

25

I accept, acknowledge, believe in, and embrace the proven power of prayer to aid in my healing process.

Healing Actions

Here are three things you can do, starting today, to help you more effectively receive the incredible benefits of prayer.

1. Pray every day

Learn two or three healing prayers that resonate with you and speak them, silently or audibly, at least two or three times a day. Speak them with love. Speak them with hope and positive expectation. Speak them with gratitude. Put your heart and soul into it.

2. Form a prayer circle

Ask everyone you can to form a prayer circle to pray on your behalf at one or two scheduled times during the day throughout your hospitalization or illness as well as at the exact time of any surgery, procedure, or infusion you may undergo. Provide them with a sample or two, expect the very best from them, and maintain a grateful spirit at all times.

3. Believe!

Remember that the power of prayer in healing has been proven in hundreds upon hundreds of studies. So, believe in it. Embrace it. And expect the very best from your prayer and those of your loved ones.

12

Get Weller Sooner with the Power of Love

"Eventually you will come to understand that love heals everything, and that love is all there is."

Gary Zukav

"Being deeply loved by someone gives you strength, while loving someone deeply gives you courage."

Laozi

Love is a many-splendored thing.

No argument there! Love is, most assuredly, a many-splendored thing. I'm sure you would agree that, if we were to conduct a worldwide survey, we would find a virtually universal consensus that love is simply the best thing we Earthlings have going for ourselves.

And, if you strip away all the trappings of our ego-driven existence—money, achievement, status, beauty, and so on—you realize that love is not only the best thing we have; it is all we have.

Now, of course, we're not just talking about romantic love, but, rather, love in all its forms: Love of self, family, children, God, nature, animals, good music, a good book, good food, and life itself, to name a few. There is a world of stuff to love in this life of ours. And there is no denying its incredible and very versatile power—including, at this juncture, its amazing power to help get your butt out of that hospital.

> ***If you sincerely want to get weller sooner, take full advantage of love's amazing power to heal.***

Once again, you have western medicine on your side—yes, even here—even regarding what had once been such a non-quantifiable, non-science-based, touchy-feely commodity as love. Quantifiable or not, science can no longer deny the fact that love heals. It just does, no matter what the cause or reason.

Dean Shrock, Ph.D., author of *Why Love Heals*, who was Director of Mind-Body Medicine for numerous cancer centers, discovered through research that his patients enjoyed a much higher survival rate than was typical for people in similar straits. However, it wasn't his programs that did it. His research concluded that it was, more than anything else, a result of his loving and compassionate nature toward his patients. They felt cared for and truly loved by him.

As he explained it: "Love is oneness. We are, on a subatomic level, all connected."

Or, as Dr. Leonard Lasko put it: "All disease comes from a perceived sense of separation."

"All disease comes from a perceived sense of separation."

So, yes, of course, love's power to heal has been vetted in study after study. An increasing number of wise and compassionate doctors are near to the point of writing prescriptions for oxytocin—the "hormone of love"—to their patients.

After all, if all disease does arise from a perceived sense of separation, then it would seem to me that feelings of love, being the antithesis of a feeling of separation, would do a good job of helping to rid one's body of disease.

So, in that spirit, consider this chapter to be your prescription for a maximum dose of "love consciousness" to be added to your daily healing and recovery regimen.

Why? First of all, loving and being loved relieves stress. This allows your body to focus on healing.

Next, having people to love gives us something to fight for. We don't give up; we don't give in; we hang in there. Having people to love means that we matter, we are needed. This is huge. Having someone or something to fight for makes us very strong; in many cases, it can spell the difference between life and death.

Finally, love is *energy* (but you already knew that, right?). It is the most powerful energy in the Universe and, thus, it is hardwired into your body chemistry. Love is everywhere in your body—assuming, of course, that you are in a loving state. It flows through *all* of you. It flows throughout you.

In a sense, because it occupies so much of you, and influences so much of you, it could well be said that love *is* you. Physically, emotionally, and spiritually: *Love is you.*

This being the case, you don't need to be a doctor or a scientist to understand that if you have the most powerful, positive, and life-sustaining energy flowing throughout your body, you *will,* in no uncertain terms, get better. It is a given.

> **If you have the most powerful, positive, and life-sustaining energy in the Universe flowing throughout your body, you will heal.**

Now, let's turbocharge that power to the max and squeeze every drop of healing we can get out of the incredible power of love. Here are some ways to heighten your feeling of love consciousness and increase the height, depth, and breadth of your loving spirit:

Connect.

Feel and foster a deep and genuine sense of connectedness—of quantum connectedness—with all. According to quantum science, everything in the Universe is connected anyway, right? So, you might just as well feel it—to the hilt.

Feel a deep sense of connection with your family and friends, of course, but also with all fellow humans with whom you share this planet. Just make the choice to feel a physical, emotional, and spiritual connection with everyone. Feel close to people in general. Feel a bond. Feel "one" with everyone. Do this simply by *choosing* to do it.

As I've said many times throughout this book, we are energy. So, it is easy to feel your energy merge or interface with the energy of everyone else. In fact, in this regard, you really don't have to "do" anything. As long as you are *feeling* love toward someone, your energies will merge on their own. Since matter, including that which makes up our bodies, is not solid, there are no barriers, no solid walls. Energies simply mesh together, if they are so directed.

Touch.

If you want to feel deeply connected with someone, the most direct way to do so is through touch—touching and being touched. We are biologically wired to thrive through touch. This need not be romantic or even affectionate contact. Simple casual touch—a brush of hands, a hand on a shoulder, a quick hug, a peck on the cheek. It's all beneficial. Touch appropriately, of course, but do touch often—and welcome the same from others.

Speaking of hugging: when the opportunity arises, lose yourself in a good, lingering, soothing, rejuvenating, healing hug from a friend or loved one whenever you can. Ask if you must; there is nothing wrong whatsoever with saying,

"I sure could use a hug right now," especially when you are ill, facing surgery, or recovering from surgery.

And when you do get to enjoy a good, long hug, really savor it. Feel its beautiful energy flow inside you. Feel that hug with your entire being. Feel yourself being soothed, comforted, and healed by it. Savor it. Languish in it. Luxuriate in it. Now, that's medicine!

We *are* energy. So, when you touch in any way, know that, in a very real sense, touch is not merely skin-deep.

Give.

A loving spirit is a giving spirit. Most of the healing and physiological benefits that arise from the power of love do so through the act of giving it. Receiving it sure feels nice too. And perhaps the more you give, the more you will ultimately get back. But even in situations when it is not reciprocated, that's perfectly fine. Know that it is the *giving* of love from which your healing will benefit most.

This form of love is often referred to as *agape*. Agape is a very all-encompassing, compassionate, goodwill-infused, and generous form of love that is separate from romantic love and even love of family. It is when you feel a bond of connection to all life, to all of nature, and you act upon this connection by appreciating the many recipients of your love and by giving of yourself to them, even if all you can manage to give right now is your respect, concern, and goodwill. Agape is pure *good*. And it is unquestionably good for you.

And speaking of *you*...

Don't forget to love yourself. Please. If you haven't made it a habit over the years to love yourself, make the choice, right now, to change that. Just choose to love yourself. Every so often, whisper *"I love you"* to yourself. It might feel a bit odd at first, but I promise you'll get used to it.

A body and a being will undeniably strive and thrive better when it is loved—especially when it is the recipient of love from its owner.

A body and a being will strive and thrive better when it is loved—especially when it is the recipient of love from its owner.

Live.

Be a lover of life itself! Love the feeling of being alive—even when you feel like crap. Love the miracle—the true miracle—of life. Embrace life joyfully, gratefully, deeply, and completely.

Thoroughly embrace it. Don't think for one second that a spirit in love with life will not, in some manner, send healing energy to the rest of the body.

All of this may sound like a lot—especially when you are sick or weak or in pain. But it is precisely during these times when you need the healing power of love the most. So, if all you can manage during this time is to feel deep, unconditional love for the people around you—family, friends, physicians, nurses, technicians, and fellow patients—and think on that love, and embrace that love, and feel grateful for that love, it will be enough. Just take the opportunity to feel love toward whomever you are near, and it will be enough.

Giving love to others—through thought, feeling, or action—truly is the greatest gift you can give yourself when you are in the process of getting weller sooner. You will heal from the giving—quickly, completely, and effortlessly. And, if you may be so fortunate as to get some love in return, well, we can only imagine how much you will thrive!

Affirm the Healing Power of Love

Read the following affirmations, silently or aloud, *with conviction and feeling.*

1

My loving connection to the people around me, my fellow man, and the world at large is very strongly linked to my healing and recovery process, as well as my long-term prospects for good health and well-being.

2

I treasure my family relationships, and I value my close friendships.

3

I love all the little things that make my life great: Music, film, food, animals, birds, sunshine, rain, a good book, a cup of tea. I have so much to look forward to!

4

I am in love with life. I am deeply, truly, joyfully, and zestfully in love with life.

5

I love myself—and this includes the miracle of my amazing body.

6

My heart, mind, and spirit are ever-filled with loving, healing, sustaining energy.

7

I am loving, and I am lovable.

8

I spend a good amount of time reflecting on all the wonderful, caring people in my life and feeling grateful for every one of them.

9

My loving spirit heals my body. My loving spirit empowers my body. My loving spirit keeps me going.

10

I am warm and good-natured. I am kind and pleasant. I am personal and cordial. I am friendly and sociable. I am affable and amicable.

11

I feel the warm, healing tingle of love energy flowing throughout my body whenever I am with, or simply thinking about, a loved one.

12

I have so many people and so many other blessings in my life to love. I have so much to live for and so much to fight for.

13

I feel the loving energy from my family and friends merge with the loving energy within my own body, making it stronger, healthier, and more vital than ever.

14

I understand that, when I feel too sick, tired, or in pain to feel love, this is when I need to feel it the most.

15

I choose to love the people in my life more deeply and more demonstratively than ever.

16

Right now, I am infusing every cell in my body with the energy of my loving spirit.

17

My body is ever healed and renewed by the love I hold in my heart. My heart is renewed with the same love.

18

I understand that to love much is to live strong and long.

19

I am grateful for the love that fills my being—both from my own heart as well as the hearts of others.

20

I send out sincere, heartfelt vibrations of love to everyone I meet, expecting nothing in return.

21

When I am in pain, recovering from surgery, receiving an infusion, or undergoing treatment, I focus the entirety of my mind on everything in my life that I love.

22

I value the importance of touch regarding my health and my emotional well-being.

23

I understand that to love—deeply and unconditionally—is one of the most beneficial things I can do for my health and well-being.

24

I love this beautiful world of ours. I love the splendor and majesty of nature. I love all creation.

25

I accept, acknowledge, and believe in, and embrace the power of my loving spirit to aid in my healing process.

Healing Actions

As has often been said, love is a verb. It isn't just a feeling you have; it is something you *do*. Here are three things you can do, starting today, to help maximize the healing power of love throughout your being.

1. Make a list

Using a note-taking app on your phone, or simple pen and paper, list all the things you love. Here are some prompts to get you started: Your family, friends, children, pets, God, your hobbies, favorite foods, travel, nature, favorite music, movies, TV shows, books. Take some time with this. Be thorough. Now see? You do have a lot to fight for, a lot to feel rejuvenated, strengthened, and healed by. Embrace, enjoy, and love all of them.

2. Be an insufferable hugger

Seek out and offer up hugs—both quick and lingering—from anyone you can. Enjoy these direct and powerful infusers-of-healing as much as you can.

3. Create a whole new point of view

Regardless of how loving a person you may already be, just make the decision right now to more deeply embrace the people and the world around you with your genuine loving spirit. Be a lover of life. Be a loving liver of life.

Putting It All Together

"Your positive action, combined with positive thinking, results in success."
Shiv Khera

"The key to success is action, and the essential in action is perseverance."
Sun Yat-sen

So, how are you feeling? Weller yet? I sure hope so. But whether the twelve healing methods you've just learned have begun to improve and accelerate your healing yet or not, I have found that it is usually easier to better understand and internalize something if I have a broad overview of the material and make sure that I understand the key points.

To that end, let's briefly go over the twelve healing methods so that you may better absorb the key takeaway points from each.

1. The Power of Your Mind

The power of the mind-body connection is more profound and more incredible than most people realize. Because everything is made of energy, and energy is made from awareness (thought), your thought-energy has a direct and powerful effect upon the very energy that makes up your body. Your body is, to no small degree, as healthy, or as unhealthy, as you think it is. You will, to no small degree, heal as well, or as poorly, as you think it will.

You are in charge of your healing. Recognize and call upon the incredible power your thinking has upon your body's ability to heal, as well as its overall state of health.

2. The Power of Positive Thinking

Since your thinking strongly influences your body, including its ability to heal, it is vitally important to keep your thoughts regarding your body, your health, and your prospects for recovery and healing one-hundred percent positive.

Think only the best thoughts about your body. Think only the best thoughts about your healing and recovery. Think only the best thoughts period.

3. The Power of Positive Expectation

Your expectations impact your health and healing to such a high degree that these expectations drive virtually every medical outcome you will ever have. First, keeping your expectations positive will improve your recovery tremendously. Second, expecting the most and the best from every other healing method in this book will increase its power to help make you well.

Expect the best in regards to your body. Expect to heal. Expect to remain healthy thereafter. Expect the best possible outcome from every healing strategy you've learned in this book.

4. The Power of Inner Strength

You need inner strength to fight and overcome any medical challenge. You can't let an illness or surgery set you back. You can't let it defeat you. You must be strong—mentally, emotionally, and physically—and it all starts with inner strength. You access your deep reserves of inner strength simply by summoning it; by calling upon it.

Know that inner strength is something that resides in all of us. Be strong simply by calling upon your inner strength and know that it will be there for you.

5. Becoming the Perfect Patient

Acting as the perfect patient—one who is pleasant to everyone involved in your care and who follows your doctor's suggestions to the letter—surrounds you in good karma, and good karma will come back to you. One way or another, it will benefit your healing.

You reap what you sow. Be the perfect patient. Be the patient who everyone likes and admires. Put out nothing but good, pleasant, friendly, positive, cooperative energy throughout your healing and recovery process.

6. The Power of Laughter

Laugher is so instrumental in the healing process and so easy to obtain nowadays, there is no excuse for not calling upon this proven healing technique.

Using the power of the Internet (YouTube, XM Radio, Pandora, etc.), access all the comedy you can, in whatever form tickles you most. Call upon this proven healing strategy and laugh yourself to a speedier recovery.

7. The Power of Music

The same goes for music. It is so easy to obtain and enjoy nowadays, that there is no excuse for not adding to your healing regimen. Music's power to heal has been scientifically proven, and it is of extreme value in the healing process.

Make playlists of soothing, healing music and listen to them incessantly throughout your illness, before and after surgery, and even while you are under anesthesia. There can be a no more enjoyable way of getting weller sooner.

8. The Power of Affirmation

Repeating positive statements about a desired outcome is used by many of the greats in all fields. Affirmations work. But, as well as they work in matters outside the body, such as the building of wealth or success, they are even more effective in matters regarding your own body, over which you have tremendous control.

Repeat the positive healing affirmations in Chapter 8 incessantly. Take this one big step further and come up with some of your own. Infuse their powerful healing energy into your being as often as you possibly can.

9. The Power of Good Nutrition

You are what you eat. Every cell in your body is something you ate within the past seven years' time. Good food is *the* way of healing in many situations.

Eat only real food: Natural, organic, minimally processed food. Think plants and lean meat. Eat the very best you can no matter what your circumstances may be. Go the extra mile by believing in the power of the food you eat to make you well.

10. The Power of Medicine

Like placebos, real medicines tend to work to the extent that you believe in their power to do so—and they do it better.

Believe—deeply believe—in the power of any medicines given or prescribed to you. Know that they will work exactly as directed and they will be far more likely to do so. Trust in your doctor's ability to choose the perfect medication for you.

11. The Power of Prayer

Prayer works, and it has been proven to work in over a thousand scientific studies. Embrace it with all your heart.

Pray for your healing daily, and bring together a prayer circle of friends and loved ones to pray for your rapid recovery. Don't miss out on this one!

12. The Power of Love

Love is everything. Love is all-powerful. A loving spirit is a healing spirit. To love much is to live well and to be well.

Be a lover of life and a lover of all. Make the decision to maintain a loving spirit now and into the future. Feel love deeply and completely, now and into the future.

Your Daily Healing Regimen

Please recite the following twelve affirmations as often as you possibly can. They bring this whole book together in the most succinct form possible. You've only to infuse the teachings into your heart and then act upon them.

1

I understand the true depth of the mind-body connection. My thoughts are energy. My body is energy. I think strength, good health, and wellness always and, in so doing, I infuse my body with strength, good health, and wellness.

2

I recognize the power of positive thinking in matters of healing and recovery. I choose to keep my thoughts happy, hopeful, and upbeat. In so doing, I am filling my physical being with these powerful, good-health-inducing energies.

3

The power of positive expectation improves all facets of my healing process. Throughout this time of illness, surgery, or treatment, I expect nothing but the best from my body, my medical team, my medicine, and from all the steps I have learned from this book on how to get weller sooner.

4

I am well aware that inner strength is vital to my speedy recovery. I have all the inner strength I need simply by my choosing to call upon it from within.

5

I understand that, by acting as the perfect patient, I am sending forth positive karma that will, in some way, return to me in the form of improved healing. I remain cheerful, upbeat, and cooperative toward all members of my medical team, knowing that this positive, outgoing energy will, in some way, manifest as an improvement in my condition.

6

I fully understand that the ability of laughter to aid in healing is well documented. I seek out sources of laughter across the Internet as part of my healing regimen.

7

I fully understand that the ability of music to aid in healing is well documented. I listen to beautiful, soothing music at every opportunity as part of my daily healing regimen.

8

The repetition of positive healing statements goes a long way in helping me to heal more quickly and completely. I repeat healing affirmations every day; I do so with conviction and with the firm belief that they will aid in my healing process.

9

Good food nourishes my body, builds my body, and heals my body. I eat the very best food I can get to help speed my recovery.

10

I understand that the power of medicine to heal is greatly enhanced by my expectation that it will work. I take all medications with unwavering faith that they will work precisely as promised.

11

I am well aware that the power of prayer to heal is well documented. I pray every day for my healing, and I am blessed with a circle of loved ones who pray every day on my behalf.

12

I recognize love as the most powerful healing force in the Universe. Even while ill or recovering from surgery, I remain a lover of life, and I feel a deep connection with, and gratitude for, my loved ones.

And that, as they say, is that. Do your work and may the forces both inside your body and outside coalesce into the most incredible healing power you've ever experienced.

Get well soon. Better yet, get weller sooner—and the sooner, the better!

* * * *

Dear Reader,

Thank you so much for reading this book! I hope you enjoyed it and found it helpful.

Might I ask you to consider writing an honest review for this book? This will help me to continue writing books that help my readers to improve the quality of their lives. It will also help future readers to make informed decisions about which books to add to their collection. Please take a moment to return to the web site where you purchased this book and leave your review for others. And, of course, spreading the word about this book to your friends would be *greatly* appreciated.

Thanks in advance and may you continue to get weller sooner!

Bibliography

Many thanks to the following fabulous web sites for their contributions to this book:

A mountain of thanks to <u>BrainyQuote.com</u> for most of the inspiring quotations used here.

Thanks also to the following for other great quotes:
- NotableQuotes.com
- QuoteFancy.com
- PositivelyPositive.com
- UDiscoverMusic.com
- Goodreads.com

Thanks to the following for their valuable and informative contributions:
- Moral Technologies
- Conscious Reminder
- *Quantum Healing*, by Dr. Deepak Chopra, Transworld Digital, 2010
- Mercola.com
- Scientific American
- Psychology Today
- SuccessConsciousness.com

- Cancer Treatment Centers of America
- *Humor in Medicine: Can Laughter Help in Healing?,* Allen B. Weisse, M.D., Baylor University Medical Center
- *Cassell's Dictionary of Classical Mythology,* Jenny March
- Sara Hoover, D.M.A., co-director of the Center for Music and Medicine at Johns Hopkins
- Bruce H. Lipton, PhD
- Jeanie Lerche Davis, WebMD .com
- Harold G. Koenig, M.D., Duke University, Newsmax Health
- Dean Shrock, Ph.D., author of *Why Love Heals*
- Dr. Leonard Lasko

About the Author

Stan Munslow is an author, educator, and musician. He lives in Rhode Island with his wife and his high-energy bichon maltipoo, Boo.